Turn Your Story Into Business Gold

The Ultimate Guide to Stories That Sell

Leslie Capps

WILD WOMAN MARKETING

Butterfly Books Publishing

Want to go even deeper on the concepts and master your own stories as you read?

As my way of saying, "Thank you!" for reading *Turn Your Story Into Business Gold*, I'd like to gift you the **companion Workbook**, designed to help you implement what you learn and go to the next level with your stories.

Scan the code to get it:

Turn Your Story Into Business Gold: The Ultimate Guide to Stories That Sell
Copyright 2024 Leslie Capps
First Edition Published by Wild Woman Marketing in Association with Butterfly Books Publishing

Cover Design by Rob of I Love My Cover Designs
Interior Design and Typesetting by Butterfly Books Publishing

ISBN (paperback): 978-1-965652-03-9
ISBN (hardcover): 978-1-965652-04-6

Printed in the United States of America..

All Rights Reserved. This publication is licensed for your personal enjoyment only. No part of this publication may be resold, reproduced, distributed, or transmitted in any form or by any means including photocopying, recording, or other electronic or mechanical methods without the prior written permission of the publisher or author, except in the case of brief quotations embodied in reviews or certain other non-commercial uses permitted by copyright law.

www.wildwomanmarketing.com

www.butterflybookspublishing.org

Contents

Acknowledgments v

Foreword ix

Introduction: Your Story is Your Strategy for Winning Online 1

Chapter 1: The Future is Story-Driven 5

Chapter 2: Are You Speaking Your Audience's Language 23

Chapter 3: Escaping the Pitch Trap 43

Chapter 4: Crafting a Winning Pitch 59

Chapter 5: Storytelling as the Ultimate Business Tool 77

Chapter 6: Evolving Your Story as You Grow 95

Chapter 7: Stories Simplify Sales 113

Chapter 8: When a Story Becomes a Movement 131

Chapter 9: Storytelling in the Digital Era 149

Chapter 10: Mindset in Action 167

Chapter 11: Craft the Story That Only You Can Tell 185

Additional Resources 201

About the Author 203

Thank You! 205

Acknowledgments

Nothing in life, including writing a book, is ever a solo endeavor. I'm beyond grateful to everyone who played a part in this journey—your support, encouragement, and contributions made all the difference.

To my dad, who, although no longer with us, instilled in me a love for stories and the lessons they carry, holding us captive at the dinner table night after night.

To my brother, Kyle, and my mom—for being part of the foundation of my story, even in ways I didn't always realize.

To Jen and Brad, for plying me with wine, feeding me, and being the kind of neighbors everyone wishes they had.

To Jan and Paul, for making sure that writing a book for the Oscars didn't go to my head—and to Pat, who offered a fancy dress for the occasion.

To Kim, for stepping in as my photographer when plans unexpectedly changed. Your support was a lifesaver.

To Karen B, for being the first to share in the excitement of the 262 book going to the Emmys and for introducing me to the General Federation of Women's Clubs—a connection that has enriched my journey.

To everyone who followed my 45-day video journey, offered comments, encouragement, and even title suggestions—thank you for showing up and inspiring me every step of the way (special shoutouts to Jeff and Yolanda).

To my amazing beta readers—Grace, Christina, Deb, Lucy, and Sharon—your thoughtful advice helped me craft a stronger story, and your encouragement kept me moving forward.

To Diane, who stepped up in the 11th inning, helping me finish the rough draft, format the manuscript, and create a table of contents—saving me so much time and sanity.

To my 262 sisters—an incredible group of women who inspire, uplift, and remind me that we're better together.

To Heather, who took a leap of faith, believing I could finish this book in time for the Oscars.

To Gloria Steinem—your voice echoes in my mind, encouraging me to speak out against injustice and always advocate for women.

To Deb Drummond—some people shorten the path, and you did that for me. I wouldn't have written this book without your encouragement and belief in me.

To Olya Z, for keeping my mindset on track and between the guardrails when things felt chaotic.

To Stephanie, for listening to every high and low along the way.

To my clients—thank you for entrusting me with your stories and inspiring me with your journeys. Your stories enriched this book in ways words can't fully express.

And to everyone who shared their personal experiences, insights, and truths along the way—your willingness to open up added depth and meaning to this book.

Finally, to everyone who played a part—thank you. This book exists because of you. If I overlooked mentioning anyone, please know it wasn't intentional—your support, no matter how small, is deeply appreciated. May this book inspire you to tell your stories, revel in others' tales, and spark meaningful connections.

Foreword

In this book, Leslie masterfully guides readers to step back and recognize the power of their life experiences. Her work encourages her readers to embrace their greatness, a quality she exudes every time you meet her.

As the creator of one of the largest platforms dedicated to helping people Show Up, Stand Up, and Speak Up in the world, I am truly amazed at how Leslie has been able to lay out such a clear, step-by-step plan for anyone to uncover the strength of their untold stories. These stories become powerful allies in amplifying your message and making your voice heard.

I've seen firsthand how sharing a story—whether on stage or in writing—can transform businesses and elevate personal confidence. Leslie's book captures this transformative magic, demonstrating how sharing your story touches hearts, changes lives, and inspires minds.

Even for those who have been sharing their stories for years and consider themselves experts, Leslie's insights will help refine and elevate their storytelling to new heights. She has truly "left it all on the table," offering lessons that will resonate with beginners and seasoned storytellers alike.

Leslie lights up every room she enters, always shining the light on others and lifting their spirits. Her big-hearted messages flow throughout these pages, and I hope you'll have the privilege of meeting her in person one day to experience her warmth and brilliance firsthand.

Leslie, you've done an incredible job creating a simple yet empowering formula for those who want their stories to be heard—those who want to use their stories to enhance their businesses or personal journeys.

It is my honor to write this foreword for Leslie. I have seen this woman make her way in the world of success with such bravery and a desire to take others with her.

I wish all of you an abundance of health, wealth, and a beautifully fulfilling life.

Be well and stay groovy,

Deborah Drummond
Top Performance Business Coach
9X International Bestselling Author
International Speaker
Motivational and Business Leader
Connect with Deb:

Introduction
Your Story is Your Strategy for Winning Online

"Your unique perspective and way of saying things – no one else can do that. That's why you will resonate and deeply impact the lives of those you're meant to."
– Katelyn Silva, We Write Books

In the business world, women are often told to tone it down, to fit into a mold. We're told to "play the game", as if success only comes when we follow the rules someone else wrote. But here's the truth: those rules were never made for us. What if we took a different approach? What if we embraced our natural strengths—storytelling, empathy, and connection—and changed what it means to "pitch like a woman"?

That's what this book is about, changing the narrative, inside and out. It's about recognizing that the journey for women in business isn't the same as it is for men. And no matter what anyone says, simple doesn't mean easy. I heard a story from a woman who was told by a male business owner, "With everything you've been through, I'd think this (business) would be easy for you." It completely threw her off. That's the problem with this kind of thinking—it assumes that because the steps are straightforward, the journey must be, too. But women know better. We know that navigating a world that wasn't built for us requires more than just following a step-by-step process—it requires intuition, grit, and resilience.

We've adapted, adjusted, and made it work in a world designed by others, for others. Now, it's time to use our voices—our stories—to change the game. Whether you're just starting out or leveling up, your story matters. It's time to stop listening to the doubts and beliefs that don't serve you and start believing in the power of your own voice.

This book is for the women who've been told they're "too much," "too emotional," or "too ambitious." It's for the women who've had to make it work in a world that wasn't designed with them in mind. It's for the women who are ready to pitch like a girl, break the mold, and own their narrative.

Think about the phrase, "You throw like a girl." You've probably heard it before, and not as a compliment. But here's the thing: it was never about how well we threw, was it? It was about comparing us to a standard that wasn't built for us. It implies that the feminine is inherently negative. This idea of "like a girl" being an insult? It's not only outdated—it's flat-out wrong.

That's why we're flipping the script. Pitching like a girl isn't something to fix; it's something to celebrate.

Introduction

Women have always been the keepers of knowledge. We pass down recipes, heal the sick, and tell the stories that connect generations. Yet in modern times, we downplay that power, especially in business. But storytelling is one of the most powerful tools in business—whether you're pitching an idea, branding yourself, or creating emotional connections with your audience.

That's where this book comes in—believing in your ability to break boundaries and pitch like a girl in a world that wasn't built for us. Growing up, my dad taught me that the story I tell myself is just as important—if not more so—than the story the world tries to impose on me.

So start there. Change the stories you tell yourself because those internal stories matter just as much as the ones you share with the world. When your internal voice aligns with your external one, you become unstoppable. Once you change the narrative inside, the world follows.

For me, Gloria Steinem has always been the voice in my head, guiding me. Gloria—an iconic leader in the feminist movement—has dedicated her life to championing equality and empowering women to embrace their voices. Her work has been my compass, reminding me to push back against outdated norms and helping me see that the power of my voice—our voices—can reshape the world around us.

Because, as you'll see, storytelling isn't just about sharing your past. It's about reclaiming your voice, owning your narrative, and using it strategically to shape the future you

Turn Your Story Into Business Gold

want. This book will guide you through the process of doing just that.

Whether you're just starting out or you've been told to "stay in your lane" one too many times, it's time to break the mold. It's time to pitch like a girl—with confidence, clarity, and the power that comes from knowing your story matters. Together, we'll unlock the tools to not only share your message but to inspire change and impact the world around you. Because when women pitch like this, the world listens.

Chapter 1
The Future is Story-Driven

"The hardest part of success is not doing the work, but keeping your head down moving forward with no guarantee of a reward in the end."
– Mads P. Rossau, Entrepreneurs Library

A multimillionaire once told me that no one cares about your story until you're successful. Let's just call BS on that right now. Your story doesn't start being important the moment you hit six figures or get featured in some fancy magazine. It's important *now*—whether you're just getting started, pivoting, or building your empire one brick at a time.

The problem is, society loves to put people—especially women—in boxes. We're told to wait until we've earned the right to speak up, to sit quietly until someone else decides we're allowed to take up space. But the truth is, our stories are constantly shaping the world around us, and they deserve to be told at every stage—messy, unfinished, or even when we feel like we're not ready.

Turn Your Story Into Business Gold

Every day, you're writing your story—whether you realize it or not. The way you show up in the world, the decisions you make, and the challenges you face all weave together into a narrative that defines you. The powerful thing about storytelling is that it's not just a reflection of your past; it's a tool to craft your future.

Think of it like this: your story is a pen, not a mirror. It's not about rehashing the past or waiting until you've checked off enough boxes to be deemed worthy of sharing. Your story is what shapes your journey moving forward, setting the tone for what's possible. So, the question isn't whether your story matters. It's whether you're ready to pick up that pen and use it.

This book is about reclaiming that pen. It's about embracing the journey you're on—whether you're just starting out or ready to level up. The stories we tell about ourselves have the power to shape our lives, our businesses, and the impact we make in the world. That's why storytelling is your greatest tool—not just for marketing, but for everything you want to build.

> *"It's the journey that makes the story so powerful."*

We're going to challenge the idea that your story only counts when you've hit the big time. In fact, it's the journey itself—the messy parts, the lessons learned, and the things no one else sees—that make your story powerful. By reclaiming your story now, you'll find the clarity, confidence, and momentum to grow into the version of yourself that you're meant to be.

Chapter 1: The Future is Story-Driven

Clues from the Past and Keys to the Future

Stories aren't just a reflection of where we've been; they leave clues about who we are and where we're going. Every story we tell contains hints of the challenges we've faced, the patterns we've repeated, and the path we're heading down. Sometimes, we get stuck in the same cycles, moving through life like robots, repeating the same patterns over and over. But storytelling has the power to disrupt those cycles.

When we take a step back and look at our stories, we see the moments that shaped us, the choices we made, and the patterns we've been unconsciously following. But more importantly, stories give us the chance to break free. They help us reframe the past, see it from a new perspective, and make different choices moving forward.

And here's where the real magic happens: stories don't just bounce us out of our own patterns, they connect us to others. When we share our stories, we're not just reflecting on our personal journey—we're opening a door for others to see themselves in our experiences. Those shared moments create powerful connections, building bridges between our struggles, our growth, and the people who need to hear our message, as well as giving them the strength to share theirs.

By telling your story, you're not only shaping your future, but also helping others break free from their own cycles. You're giving them a glimpse into what's possible—showing them that they're not alone in their journey.

The power of storytelling goes beyond just connecting us to ourselves and others—it's a critical tool in today's business landscape. From social media to sales conversations, everyone keeps saying, "You need to tell a story." But what does that mean for your business?

Defining Authentic Storytelling

Recently, an interviewer asked a question that a lot of us have wondered: "What exactly is storytelling?"

Simple enough, right? But answering it? Not so simple.

It reminded me of a conversation I saw on social media where someone asked about branding. The response was a chorus of "You've got to tell a story!"—over and over. Everyone was quick to say how important storytelling is. But when the person finally asked, "Okay, but what is a story?"—crickets.

And here's the thing—most people will tell you that you need to tell a story, but few can explain why it's important or how to actually craft one. If you've ever felt uncertain about what storytelling really means or how to use it effectively, you're in good company. In this book, we're going to break down the essentials of authentic storytelling, why it matters, and how you can start using it strategically in your business.

So, what is storytelling? We know it's important, but how do we actually do it? Where do we even start? These questions are at the heart of using your story as a strategy, and that's where many people get stuck.

Chapter 1: The Future is Story-Driven

Let's start with what storytelling *isn't*. It's not a random series of events or disconnected thoughts. It's not a list of facts or walking someone through a process step by step. Authentic storytelling has structure—a clear beginning, middle, end, and lesson—and, most importantly, it has *purpose*.

In business, you're not just telling a story for the sake of it. You're building a bridge, leading your audience from where they are to where you want them to go. But here's the thing: the story isn't about *you*. It's about them—the person listening. It's about what *they* need to hear, not just what you want to share.

We often get stuck on our own stories because, well, they're ours. We want to share our experiences with the world. But when you're telling a story for business, it's not about what matters to you—it's about what resonates with your audience. Storytelling isn't just a buzzword; it's a bridge—a connection between people; between your audience and your solution.

The Psychology of Why Stories Work

Stories resonate with people on a deep, emotional level because they create neural connections. When you tell a story, you're not just sharing information—you're forming a bond with your audience. Our brains are wired to respond to stories in unique ways, different from how we take in facts or statistics. Before diving into the science, let's talk about something we all instinctively know: stories create emotional connections.

For example, if you tell someone a story about your dog and they're a dog lover, you've immediately established a bond. That's why stories are so powerful—they allow us to relate in ways facts and figures simply can't. We remember stories because they make us *feel* something, and those emotions stick with us long after the details fade.

But it's not just about emotions—there is real science behind why stories work. Researchers have found that storytelling activates specific areas in the brain, engaging us in ways that data alone cannot.

Neural Coupling: How Stories Sync Brains

Research from Princeton University, led by Uri Hasson, shows that when someone tells a story, the listener's brain starts to mirror the storyteller's brain activity. This phenomenon, called neural coupling, creates a deep connection between the storyteller and the listener.[1] Essentially, when you tell a story, your brain and the listener's brain sync up, making it easier for them to understand and remember your message. That's just one way that storytelling builds connection.

The Power of Oxytocin: Building Trust Through Stories

Paul Zak, a neuroeconomist from Claremont Graduate University, found that stories that elicit emotional responses trigger the release of oxytocin, the "trust

---

[1] Hasson, U., Ghazanfar, A. A., Galantucci, B., Garrod, S., & Keysers, C. (2012). Brain-to-brain coupling: A mechanism for creating and sharing a social world. Trends in Cognitive Sciences, 16(2), 114–121. https://doi.org/10.1016/j.tics.2011.12.007.

Chapter 1: The Future is Story-Driven

hormone."[2] Oxytocin is responsible for feelings of empathy and trust. When someone listens to a well-crafted, emotionally engaging story, their brain releases oxytocin, making them more likely to trust you and take action. This is why stories are so effective in business—they build trust quickly without hard-sell tactics.

Stories engage multiple areas of the brain, which makes them more memorable than simply presenting information. When we listen to a story, our sensory, motor, and emotional areas light up. This increased brain activity is why people remember stories far better than they remember data or facts. It's the reason you can recall the plot of a movie from years ago but not the numbers from last week's presentation.

Beyond building trust and engagement, stories also simplify complex ideas. In a world full of noise—social media posts, ads, and endless marketing funnels—a clear, compelling story cuts through the chaos. When people can see themselves in your story, the connection becomes even stronger.

This is why stories are foundational to any business strategy their power to build connections makes them invaluable tools for sales and marketing. Rather than overwhelming your audience with details, a story invites them into a narrative where

> *Stories build trust, simplify complex ideas, and help others connect more deeply.*

---

[2] Zak, P. J. (2015). Why inspiring stories make us react: The neuroscience of narrative. Cerebrum: The Dana Forum on Brain Science. Retrieved from Dana Foundation.

they see themselves as the hero. It helps them relate to your message on a personal level, making the story feel like their own.

Ultimately, stories work because they build trust, simplify complex ideas, and help your audience connect with you on a deeper level.

Stories with Intention

In business, storytelling has to be more than just an emotional tale—it needs a clear goal and intention behind it. Think of your story like a roadmap. It's not enough to take someone on a journey; you need to lead them to a specific destination. Your story should always move people toward something—a lesson, an action, or a change in perspective.

That matters because sales are made on emotion. People don't buy based on logic; they buy based on feelings. The facts? Those come later, to justify the decision they've already made. The emotional connection drives the sale. That's why storytelling is such a powerful tool in business. It allows you to create an open door, inviting people into your world authentically, without feeling forced or "salesy."

The aggressive, hard-sell tactics often associated with a car salesman are outdated, and most women and many men find this style uncomfortable. We don't want to be in people's faces, telling them what they need. Instead, storytelling lets us connect with empathy. It's about offering a slice of who we are and showing how we can help—without being pushy or overbearing.

Storytelling makes you memorable. The clearer and more defined your story is, the easier it is for people to remember you and what you do. If your story is vague or confusing, people won't understand how to refer you to others who might need your help. I once spent forty-five minutes talking to someone, and by the end, I still had no idea how I could refer to them. Clarity in your story not only helps people connect with you, but it opens doors to opportunities you might otherwise miss.

Once you clarify your intention, it's time to address how your story shapes something even bigger—your brand. Whether you're running a small business or building an empire, your story is the foundation of what people will remember about you.

Your Story is Your Brand—Regardless of Size

Every business, no matter how small, has a brand—and at the heart of that brand is your story. Whether you're running a solo operation or leading a global company, the story you tell becomes the foundation of your brand identity. It's what people remember long after the facts and figures fade.

Take David, a business coach who struggled to connect with his audience on LinkedIn. He knew his ideal clients were there, but he couldn't reach them. Frustrated by this gap, David created a solution called the "LinkedIn Concierge" to make genuine connections easier. But, when he tried to explain his solution, he focused so heavily

Turn Your Story Into Business Gold

on the technical details that he overlooked the story that inspired it.

Once we shifted David's focus back to his own struggles and the solution he developed, his audience began to understand *why* he developed the LinkedIn Concierge. That story became a bridge building trust with his audience. With that trust, he created a foundation for a thriving business.

For small businesses or individual entrepreneurs, it's easy to assume branding is only for companies like Apple or McDonald's. But that's not true. If anything, your story matters more because *you* are the brand. People aren't just buying a product—they're buying you, your services, and your expertise.

Look at McDonald's. It didn't become a global giant overnight. Ray Kroc didn't just sell hamburgers—he sold a vision of consistency and efficiency, a place where people always knew what to expect. That story of reliability became McDonald's enduring brand. And even today, long after Kroc's time, the golden arches continue to tell that story.

The same principle applies to you, even if you're a single-owner business. Your brand is a reflection of who you are—your values, your mission, and the solutions you provide. People don't buy from faceless companies; they buy from people they trust. Your story is the key to building that trust and establishing your brand identity.

Even Apple, now a huge, international brand, began with Steve Jobs in a garage. He wasn't just building products—

Chapter 1: The Future is Story-Driven

he was creating a brand that stood for innovation, design, and breaking boundaries. His vision and values became the DNA of Apple, and today, every iPhone connects us to Jobs' original story of blending function and beauty.

Maybe you won't grow into an Apple or McDonald's, and that's okay. The point is that every brand, no matter the size, starts with a single person and a story. What problem are you solving? What values drive your business? When you can clearly communicate that story, your audience will understand what you stand for, and your brand will resonate deeply with the right people.

Branding isn't just about logos or colors. Those elements are meaningless without a story behind them. Your brand is the story you tell about who you are and the values you stand for. If that story is clear, people will remember you, trust you, and want to work with you. If it's vague or confusing, they'll move on.

Your brand reflects the story you tell the world, but as your vision and goals expand, your story needs to grow with it. It's not just about what you've built so far—it's about the bigger mission you're stepping into.

The Bigger You Think, the More You Grow

The story you tell is more than just a reflection of your business—it's the foundation of your potential. If you cling to an outdated narrative or play small, you'll limit your growth. Your story needs to evolve as your vision expands, reflecting the bigger mission and future you're stepping into.

I've seen this happen time and time again with clients. Janet, for example, felt stuck calling herself a "brand photographer." She knew she was passionate about capturing moments, but it wasn't until she shared the real reason behind her work that things clicked.

A family member was dying, and Janet realized how important it was to create lasting memories. That vulnerability became the heart of her 'why'. Once she started telling that story, she didn't have to explain how she approached her clients' branding photos—it was already understood. Her story did the heavy lifting, and the business came pouring in.

When you lean into the deeper aspects of your story, you stop playing small. You're not just selling a product or service—you're sharing the real reason behind what you do. That's what resonates with people on a human level. They don't just want to buy from you—they want to be part of your story.

Seeking Outside Guidance

As entrepreneurs, we can get so wrapped up in our own stories that we lose sight of what really resonates. We guard our version of events fiercely, and that's exactly when outside guidance becomes a game changer. Sometimes, all it takes is the right coach or mentor to cut through the fog and show us what we're missing.

I worked with a client who had been stuck for over a year, spinning in circles with a coach who couldn't help him move forward. He served two different types of clients and couldn't figure out how to speak to both on his website. He thought he had to pick one audience or the other. I offered a simple shift: create two separate funnels with distinct sales pages for each. Boom—clarity. Suddenly, he could talk to both sets of clients without confusion, and the money started rolling in.

Another client came to me frustrated because his title—CFO (chief financial officer)—wasn't cutting it. It was so vague that he'd end up spending twenty minutes trying to explain what he really did, at which point his audience had checked out. We cleaned up his messaging, zeroing in on what mattered: helping businesses find hidden cash and eliminate unnecessary losses. Suddenly, people got it. He went from "just another CFO" to a cash strategist, and with that clarity, he spent more time getting results and less time explaining himself.

Outside guidance doesn't just give you solutions—it brings clarity. The right coach can help you step back, see the bigger picture, and guide you toward a narrative that reflects who you really are and where you're going. Often, the biggest breakthroughs come when someone helps you break free from the story that's been holding you back.

Sometimes, it takes someone else's perspective to help us step into the bigger version of ourselves. This book serves as that guide, helping you see your story through fresh eyes and crafting a narrative that leads to greater impact.

Why Storytelling Matters in Business

Storytelling isn't just about getting your message out—it's

about creating a connection that sticks. In today's crowded market, your product or service alone isn't enough to stand out. People want to do business with those they trust, and trust is built on shared experiences and emotions. That's where your story comes in.

Take, for example, the businesses that shifted from traditional sales pitches to story-driven marketing. They didn't just talk about what they offered—they talked about *why* they did it, how they overcame challenges, and the impact they've had. That emotional resonance changes everything. Suddenly, clients aren't just buying a product; they're buying into the person behind the brand. And once that trust is built, loyalty follows.

But it's not just about standing out. Storytelling simplifies communication. Instead of bombarding potential clients with data or long-winded explanations, a clear story helps them *see* themselves in the narrative. It answers the unspoken question: "What's in it for me?" in a way that's natural and engaging.

A good story also makes your brand memorable. Think of brands like Nike or Apple. Their success isn't just about their products—it's about the powerful narratives they've built around them. Apple doesn't just sell tech; they sell innovation and creativity. Nike doesn't just sell shoes; they sell the belief that anyone can be an athlete. Those stories connect on a personal level, turning customers into loyal advocates.

For small businesses, the impact of storytelling can be even greater. When you share a personal, authentic story, you humanize your brand. It becomes more than just a transaction—it becomes a relationship. And when clients feel connected to you, they're not only more likely to buy, but they're also more likely to refer you to others.

Conclusion

Your story isn't just a part of your brand—it *is* your brand. It's the thread that runs through everything you do, the foundation that sets you apart, and the reason people connect with you. But more than that, it's your greatest asset in shaping the future of your business and your life.

You have the power to shape a narrative that moves beyond what's been holding you back, beyond the smaller version of yourself you may have been telling. Your story is the key to unlocking the potential you already have—the doors you didn't realize were waiting to open. And it's not just about business success; it's about stepping into the full version of who you're meant to be.

As we continue through this book, we'll unpack how to use storytelling to not only grow your business, but to expand your influence, create deeper connections, and lead with intention. The tools are here, but the most important thing you bring to the table is your story. It's unique, it's powerful, and it's time for the world to hear it.

So, ask yourself: What story do you want to live? Because that's the point of this journey—crafting the narrative that reflects the future you're building. It's not just about where you've been; it's about where you're going, and how your story will take you there.

Key Takeaways

1. **Your Story Is Your Most Powerful Asset:** Your story is the foundation of your brand and the key to connecting with your audience. It sets you apart and creates the emotional connection that drives trust and business growth.

2. **Strategic Storytelling Drives Action**: Storytelling with intention guides your audience toward specific outcomes, whether it's building trust, driving sales, or creating lasting relationships. Every story you tell in business should have a clear purpose.

3. **Embrace a Bigger Story for Bigger Growth:** To grow your business, step into a bigger version of your story. When you expand your vision and own a bolder narrative, you open doors to opportunities and success you didn't realize were possible.

4. **Outside Perspectives To Uncover Hidden Strengths:** Sometimes, we're too close to our stories to see the full potential. Seeking guidance from a coach or mentor can reveal the strengths and opportunities you've been overlooking and help you shift your narrative toward greater impact.

Mindset Shifts

1. **From Safety to Boldness:** Instead of sticking to the familiar version of your story, embrace the discomfort of stepping into a bigger, more ambitious narrative.

Chapter 1: The Future is Story-Driven

2. **From Past Focus to Future Vision:** Shift from relaying the past to intentionally crafting a story that reflects where you're headed. Your story is not just a record of your past; it's a tool to shape your future success.

3. **From Judgment to Owning:** Stop worrying about how others will perceive your story or whether it's "too much." Recognize that your story has the power to inspire, lead, and drive real change. The more authentic and bold you are, the more impact you'll have.

Action Steps

1. **Reflect on Your Current Story:** Write down the story you're telling yourself and others about your business. Identify where you need to expand or refine your narrative.

2. **Identify a Key Experience to Share:** Choose a specific moment in your business journey—whether a challenge or a success—that could resonate with your audience. Outline how you would use this story to connect with your clients or customers and lead them toward action.

3. **Seek an Outside Perspective**: Reach out to a coach, mentor, or trusted colleague and ask them to review your current story. What strengths do they see that you might be overlooking? Use their feedback to reshape or expand.

4. **Practice Telling Your Story**: Find an opportunity this week—whether in a meeting, a social media post, or a client conversation—to intentionally tell your story. Focus on creating a connection and delivering a clear message that guides your audience to the outcome you want.

If you haven't yet gotten your complimentary companion Workbook to go deeper and actually write our your thoughts, shifts, and steps, scan the code to get it now:

Chapter 2
Are You Speaking Your Audience's Language

"Share your story with style! It's the spark that opens hearts, unlocks grace, and opens doors to connections and self-discovery unfolding like a grand adventure."
– Grace C.W. Liu, Truth Empowerment Navigator

We all know that understanding our audience is critical in business, especially in the online space. But it goes way beyond just knowing their age, gender, or lifestyle. Sure, those things matter, but they barely scratch the surface. If you really want to connect with your audience, you've got to tap into their emotions, desires, and fears—the things that truly drive their decisions.

In this chapter, we're digging deep into what it means to *really* know your audience—not just on a surface level, but understanding what makes them tick. We'll talk about how to uncover their pain points, speak their language, and create stories that hit home. It's about positioning yourself as the guide who takes them from where they are now to where they want to be.

By the time we're done, you won't just have a clearer picture of who your audience is—you'll know how to create messages and stories that speak straight to their hearts. And when you do that? Trust builds, relationships grow, and so does your business.

There's Power in Knowing Your Audience

Speaking the language of your audience is where magic happens. Once you've identified your ideal client, pay close attention to the words and phrases they use. What are they asking about? What's keeping them up at night? One of the best ways to do this is by a little *cyber-stalking*—follow them on social media, read their posts, observe the questions they ask, and take note of their language.

After a presentation I gave recently, the questions people asked were a goldmine. Different people were asking similar things in different ways, which told me there was a specific topic they wanted more clarity on. This kind of feedback helped me shape my future content such as presentations, blog posts, or content for social media.

When I speak directly to my audience's specific questions and concerns, I'm able to connect with people on a deeper level. They feel heard. They'll think, "Wow, she knows exactly what I'm going through." This happens on a subconscious level, but it builds trust and turns casual readers into loyal clients.

Chapter 2: Are You Speaking Your Audience's Language?

Let's take it a step further: when you reflect your audience's fears, desires, and goals back to them in their own language, they feel seen and understood. And here's the thing—your audience wants a solution, but they also want to be heard. When your messaging mirrors what's already in their minds, they'll be more open to how you can help—and trust that you can.

With insights into where your audience spends time online, the questions they're asking, and the words they use, you can create stories that speak directly to them and their needs. And if you're not sure where to start, don't worry—we'll cover that in the chapters ahead. See how I just addressed your concerns? Yeah, I'm clever like that!

Here's what we're aiming for: take dull messaging that sounds like everyone else—"We offer comprehensive marketing services to help businesses grow their online presence"—and turn it into something like, "Struggling to get noticed online? We help overwhelmed entrepreneurs build a standout digital presence—without the chaos."

That second statement? *Boom*—it hits home. It speaks to the exact problem and offers a solution without sounding generic or boring.

Avoid Over-Explaining the "How"

It's crucial to position yourself as the expert—the person with the shortcut to solve your audience's problems—but you need to resist getting bogged down in the technical details. Your audience doesn't need the nitty-gritty of how

Turn Your Story Into Business Gold

you do things; they just need to trust that you can solve their problem.

It's easy to slip into the habit of explaining every detail of your process, but that often leads people to tune out. Instead, focus on what you can do for your clients. Think about it—just like how teenagers roll their eyes at a long-winded explanation, clients don't want the step-by-step breakdown. They want to feel understood and to know that you have the solution. By prioritizing their needs over your process, you'll hold their attention and demonstrate your ability to deliver results.

> *Your audience doesn't want long explanations. They want to feel seen and understood.*

We're all juggling bigger priorities than listening to a detailed account of how things work. If you hire a carpenter to build a closet, you're not interested in the specific tools or every step of the process—you just want assurance that, by the end, you'll have a beautiful space for your shoes and cocktail dresses. Trust me, building a closet has more moving parts than you think, but hearing about them is tedious.

Let's be real—most solutions involve multiple steps, but no one gets excited about a long, drawn-out explanation. I once met someone at a networking event who introduced himself by saying he helps people build six-figure businesses through financial analysis, blah blah blah... and I completely tuned out. Why? He focused too much on the "how" instead of what he could actually do for me.

Chapter 2: Are You Speaking Your Audience's Language?

When someone gets lost in the details of the "how", it raises doubts about their confidence in delivering results. We've all experienced investing in a course or hiring a coach that didn't live up to the hype. If someone can't paint a clear picture of the transformation, we start to question whether they truly understand our needs.

That's where storytelling shines. Stories let you demonstrate your understanding of your audience's pain without needing to walk them through every step of your process. When introducing your business, don't just list what you do—share a story about a client who faced similar challenges and how you helped them transform. This approach establishes your authority while creating an emotional connection.

Let's dispel the myth that showing empathy weakens your authority. In reality, the more you demonstrate your understanding of others' struggles, the more authority you gain. Why? Because your audience feels that you genuinely get them—and that trust makes them believe in your ability to help.

I once worked with a client who felt completely overwhelmed by the idea of using storytelling in her business. She was stuck on the "how" and terrified of making mistakes. I shared my own experience of feeling the same way and how I eventually found clarity. That was the moment she trusted me—not because I laid out the process in detail, but because I understood her struggle and showed her the way through.

When Your Audience is a Mystery, It's a Minefield

We tend to generalize as a society. If something happens to one person we know, we assume it must be true for everyone. However, when it comes to your audience, that kind of thinking can lead you astray. Assuming your audience is homogeneous—lumping people together based on age, gender, or occupation—results in broad messaging that speaks to no one. While casting a big net may seem like the easy way out, it rarely works.

The reality is that people are unique. Even within the same demographic, their experiences, challenges, and desires can differ significantly. When you create generic messaging, you miss the nuances that help people feel truly understood.

We also love shortcuts—jargon, acronyms, and technical language—but that can backfire. You may be the expert in your field, but your audience speaks "human." They may not understand or care about the technical details.

I once asked a rocket scientist to explain his work, expecting to get lost in jargon. Sure enough, he launched into a long-winded explanation filled with words longer than my arm. Most audiences wouldn't have the patience for that kind of complexity. If your messaging is too technical or too broad, you risk alienating potential clients.

Saying, "I'm a life coach," doesn't convey much. However, if you say, "I help overwhelmed women create structure in their lives so they can find more time in their day," you're speaking directly to their challenges. Even if I'm not your

Chapter 2: Are You Speaking Your Audience's Language?

ideal client, I might know someone who is. Specificity fosters connection.

Seize every opportunity to ask for feedback. Whether through surveys, polls, or one-on-one conversations, getting direct input from your audience is essential. Without it, you risk creating messaging, products, or services that miss the mark. Plus, your audience will appreciate that you're listening.

Generic pain points don't cut it, either. Saying, "My audience doesn't have enough time," or, "They want more clients," is too vague. It might be true, but it lacks depth and fails to create an emotional connection. Dig deeper—are they struggling to balance work and family? Are they having trouble prioritizing tasks? Specificity breeds familiarity, which is crucial for building trust.

You've probably heard, "The riches are in the niches." Many resist niching down, fearing it will exclude potential clients. In reality, the opposite is often true. Trying to appeal to everyone results in messaging that resonates with no one. By focusing on a specific, well-defined audience, you can create deeper connections and build loyalty. Ironically, this focus often expands your reach.

Remember, your audience is more than just demographics. They are shaped by cultural, social, and even political factors. Ignoring these elements can make your messaging seem tone-deaf or out of touch. By staying aware of the

> *Speak to the one, and you will connect deeply with many.*

context in which your audience operates, you'll craft messages that feel relevant and timely.

Whether it's avoiding jargon, steering clear of generalizations, or speaking directly to your audience's specific struggles, the key is to make them feel seen. Use their language, address their unique needs, and stay engaged as those needs evolve over time.

The Client Journey From Curiosity to Conversion

If you've dipped your toes into any type of marketing, you've likely encountered the term "client journey." No, we're not talking about a leisurely road trip; every client undergoes a journey before they decide to work with you. Understanding this journey is key to using stories effectively to guide them along the way.

Here are the typical stages of a client journey:

1. **Curiosity**: This is when your audience first notices you and your brand. They might find your content intriguing or relate to the problems you're discussing, but they aren't quite ready to dive in just yet. Your job here is to spark their interest and leave a memorable impression.

2. **Connection**: As they explore more of your content, they begin to see how you could help them. This is where they start to bond with your brand. Sharing relatable stories that echo their experiences can

strengthen that connection, igniting their curiosity about what you have to offer.

3. **Trust**: Now, we reach a critical point. Your audience needs to feel confident that you understand their struggles and have the solutions they're looking for. This is when storytelling becomes a powerful tool. By sharing testimonials, case studies, or personal experiences, you can demonstrate your expertise and empathy, building the trust they need to move forward.

4. **Conversion**: Finally, it's time for action! Your audience is ready to take the plunge—whether that means purchasing your product, signing up for your service, or reaching out for more information. By this stage, they've traveled through the journey and feel assured in their choice. Clear calls to action and a smooth onboarding experience will help seal the deal.

By mapping out these stages, you can tweak your messaging and storytelling to guide your audience from curiosity all the way to conversion, making sure they feel supported and understood every step of the way.

Storytelling at Each Stage of the Client Journey

Storytelling is like a secret weapon in your marketing arsenal, and it's something you can wield at every stage of the client journey. But here's the kicker: each stage needs its own flavor of storytelling to really hit home.

Turn Your Story Into Business Gold

1. **Attracting Attention (Curiosity)**: When someone first stumbles upon your brand, they need a reason to stick around. That's where your intro story comes into play. It should be intriguing enough to spark curiosity—kind of like that cliffhanger in your favorite TV show that makes you binge-watch the next episode. You want them to feel that tingle of interest, not be bombarded with too much info right off the bat.

2. **Building Connection (Connection)**: Once you've grabbed their attention, it's time to create that connection. This is your moment to share stories that echo their struggles and dreams. By diving into their pain points and desires, you're not just another business; you're someone who gets them.

3. **Establishing Trust (Trust)**: This stage is critical. You need to show that you're the real deal. Share success stories that demonstrate your expertise—stories that say, "Hey, I've been there, and here's how I helped someone just like you." For example, I once had a client who was a whiz at getting leads on LinkedIn but struggled to articulate his value. His messaging was packed with jargon that made me feel lost. We switched gears and focused on what his clients really wanted: a hassle-free way to get more leads. Boom! He landed clients left and right once he spoke their language.

4. **Encouraging Action (Conversion)**: Now, let's talk about getting them to take action. This is where your story should paint a picture of transformation.

Chapter 2: Are You Speaking Your Audience's Language?

Your potential clients want to know if you can guide them from where they are to where they want to be. Use relatable examples to illustrate that journey, making it clear that they can achieve success with your help. Don't forget your call to action—let them know what to do next!

Stories for Each Leg of The Journey

1. Attracting Attention

At this stage, your audience is just getting to know you, so you need quick, engaging stories that spark their interest without overwhelming them. Think of these as your "hook" to pull them in.

- **Social Media Posts**: Craft short, punchy stories that highlight a key pain point your audience might be experiencing. For example, share a brief anecdote about how you helped a client overcome a common challenge, finishing with a call to action like, "Ever felt this way? Let's chat!"

- **30-Second Introduction**: When you're networking or introducing yourself online, use a quick story to convey who you are and what you do in a relatable way. For instance, "I help women juggling endless to-do lists find balance, like my client Sarah, who went from feeling overwhelmed to finding her peace in just a few weeks."

- **Website Tagline or Bio**: Create a short story or statement that gives a glimpse into your unique approach and entices people to stick around. For example, "I transform stressed-out professionals into organized powerhouses, one step at a time."

2. Building Connection

Now that you've captured their attention, it's time to use stories that show you truly understand your audience. This is all about empathy—making them feel like you get their struggles and can help them navigate them.

- **Email Newsletters or Blog Posts**: Dive into a client's challenge that reflects your audience's pain points. For example, write a blog post about how one of your clients felt overwhelmed by a flood of business advice until they found clarity with your help. This not only highlights your expertise but also shows how you can guide others facing similar obstacles.

- **Webinar or Workshop Stories:** Incorporate stories in your presentations that resonate with your audience's challenges. For instance, share how you helped a client tackle a time-management issue during a webinar on productivity. This kind of relatable storytelling can make your advice feel more actionable.

- **Instagram Stories or Reels:** Use these platforms for informal, quick stories that showcase your personality, interactions with clients or your challenges. These glimpses into your life can humanize your brand and foster a stronger connection with your audience.

3. Establishing Trust

This is where you truly build credibility. It's time to share longer, more detailed stories about your successes and the transformations you've facilitated for your clients.

- **Case Studies or Client Testimonials:** Whether on your website, in proposals, or across social media, these stories are essential for establishing trust. For example, take the LinkedIn Concierge story mentioned earlier; it showcases real results that resonate with potential clients.

- **Long-form Content** (Podcasts, Webinars, Blog Series): Use these formats to share in-depth stories about your experiences overcoming challenges or helping clients achieve their goals. For instance, a podcast episode detailing the entire journey of how you guided someone through a significant business transition can really showcase your expertise and relatability.

- **Speaking Engagements:** When you speak at events, share stories focused on client successes. This highlights your expertise while also positioning you as someone who can deliver real results. Audiences connect with stories, making your message more memorable.

4. Encouraging Action

At this stage, your audience is ready to make a decision, so your stories should highlight transformation and tangible results. They want to believe but need evidence that you can guide them from point A to point B.

- **Sales or Landing Pages:** Share a compelling story about a client who achieved a transformation similar to what your audience desires. For example, you might say, "Just like my client Anna, who doubled her income after taking our 4-hour course on simplifying her marketing strategy—you can achieve this too. Sign up today!"

- **Consultation Calls:** During one-on-one calls, weave in a relevant story that illustrates the results your clients can expect if they choose to work with you. For instance, you could share how a client faced a similar challenge and is now thriving, thanks to your guidance.

- **Email Funnels:** Craft a series of emails that narrate a client's success story step by step. Each email should nudge the reader toward taking the next action, whether that's booking a call or purchasing a service.

By leveraging these storytelling techniques, you can effectively guide your audience toward conversion. However, to ensure your stories resonate deeply, it's essential to integrate audience insights into your messaging.

Chapter 2: Are You Speaking Your Audience's Language?

Integrating Audience Insights

Your brand is more than just a logo or a catchy tagline; it's the feeling your audience gets every time they interact with you. That's why the experience should be consistent across all touchpoints. The more they encounter clear, focused messaging on various platforms, the stronger their connection to and trust in your brand will be.

Start by taking a good look at your website. Does your homepage speak to your audience's needs and desires, or is it more focused on what you do? Remember, your audience is always wondering, "What's in it for me?" Your messaging should highlight their needs and showcase the transformation you offer.

Next, consider your social media presence. Are your posts written in a way that resonates with your audience? Do they address their pain points and offer relatable solutions? When your audience can see themselves in your content, trust begins to blossom.

Emails are another key part of your brand's communication strategy. When crafting emails—whether promotional offers or newsletters—make sure the content feels personal and tailored to your audience. Keep your brand voice consistent while focusing on their desires rather than just your offers.

The goal is to create a seamless experience for your audience across all platforms. Each interaction should feel like a natural continuation of the last, reinforcing the message that you genuinely understand their struggles and are here to help them find solutions. When your messaging is clear and consistent, your audience will feel more connected to your brand, which is essential for building long-term trust.

Conclusion

Understanding your audience isn't just a checkbox on your to-do list—it's an ongoing journey and the heartbeat of your business. When you truly grasp who your audience is—their struggles, dreams, and the language they speak—you create a connection that goes beyond surface level. You won't just blend into the noise; you'll become the trusted guide they turn to for real solutions.

By focusing on their emotional journey and offering transformations instead of merely products or services, you can turn potential customers into loyal advocates. Consistency across all your platforms—be it social media, your website, or emails—reinforces that trust. Every interaction should feel personal and relevant, proving that you genuinely understand their pain points.

If you're eager to dive deeper into your clients' minds, I highly recommend conducting a comprehensive survey. It's one of the best ways to uncover the insights that can truly inform your strategy, though we can save the details for another time. For now, leverage the tools you already have—listen, observe, and stay engaged with their evolving needs.

If you find yourself feeling stuck, consider this your nudge to take the next step. Whether it's running a survey, collaborating with a coach, or simply reflecting on your

Chapter 2: Are You Speaking Your Audience's Language?

current messaging, continuous evolution is key. The more aligned you are with your audience, the more impact you'll create.

So, take everything you've learned about your audience and weave it into every aspect of your brand. Keep refining, keep learning, and always meet your audience where they are. That's where true connection happens, and that's where your business will thrive.

Key Takeaways

1. **Speak Their Language:** Understanding your audience's pain points, desires, and language is key to messaging that resonates.

2. **Focus on Transformation, Not Process:** Your audience cares more about the results you can provide than the step-by-step details.

3. **Consistency is Key:** Your messaging should be consistent across all platforms—website, social media, emails, and in-person—to build trust and connection.

4. **Stay Curious:** Audience needs evolve over time, so it's essential to continually ask and adjust your messaging and offers.

Mindset Shifts

1. **From Features to Benefits:** Shift your focus from the features of your product or service to the benefits for the client.

2. **From General to Specific:** Stop lumping people together based on demographics. Dive deep into their unique challenges and desires to speak directly to them.

3. **From Selling to Empathy:** Instead of pushing your product or service, think of how you can serve your audience's needs. Position yourself as the guide who helps them reach their desired goal, and ditch the hard sell.

Action Steps

1. **Know Your Audience:** Who is your ideal client? What keeps them up at night? What have they tried that hasn't worked? Dig into the pain and the vision.

2. **Audit Your Messaging:** Review your website, social media, and emails. Does your messaging focus on the how or the transformation? The latter delivers better results.

3. **Rewrite a Key Message:** Take one of your current marketing messages and rewrite it using your audience's language. Focus on the transformation you offer, rather than the process.

Chapter 2: Are You Speaking Your Audience's Language?

4. **Ask for Feedback:** Reach out to your audience—through surveys, polls, or one-on-one conversations—to better understand their current challenges and how you can refine your messaging.

If you haven't yet gotten your complimentary companion Workbook to go deeper and actually write our your thoughts, shifts, and steps, scan the code to get it now:

Chapter 3
Escaping the Pitch Trap

"You must displace common sense
in order to reach greatness"
– Conor Healy, Connekt Coaching

We've talked about what a story is, what it isn't, and why it's crucial to speak your audience's language. The simplest, yet ironically hardest, place to start using your story is in the pitch or introduction. You've got 30-60 seconds to hook people, but if you're not engaging, they'll mentally check out after 15. Let's dive into how to use your story to capture attention—or intentionally repel the wrong crowd.

What exactly is a pitch? In business, it's part of what I like to call "jargonology"—that's my own fancy term. A pitch can mean one of two things: the *sleazy car salesman* approach, "What's it gonna take to get you into this beauty today?" Or, at its best, it's an *introduction*—the moment you open the door to who you are, what you do, and how you can help. These two couldn't be more different, but it's easy to get them scrambled.

The first approach? That's the infamous "pitch slap." You've felt it. A conversation starts normally, and then—BAM!—you're hit with a full-on sales pitch. No connection, no context, just a hard push to close the deal. It's not just off-putting; it's a trust killer. The audience feels more like a target than a person, and instead of listening, they're mentally checking out. And the slapper never asks if you need what they're selling.

Remember our last conversation about knowing your audience? Pitch-slapping screams, "I know what you need better than you do." Naturally, people pull back and feel disconnected. **Even the person doing the pitch knows it's off,** but they push ahead anyway, hoping something will stick.

We've all been pitch slapped—and maybe, we've done it ourselves at some point. It's inauthentic and awkward, and we beat ourselves up afterward, even if we make the sale. I've been there, too—feeling the pressure to sell and letting it sneak into my words.

Recently, I had a one-on-one with someone after a networking event. She asked me where I lived and then immediately dove into her pitch. She never asked about my business. Five minutes in, she asked if I'd put her info on my website—seriously?! I barely knew what she did! It was a quick fifteen-minute conversation, but I felt completely disconnected and a little irritated. I told her I needed more info before moving forward. Her follow-up email? Full of instructions on how to add her details to my site. **Uh, thanks, but no!**

Here's the thing: **pitch-slapping** feels forced, transactional, and totally out of sync with most people's values—especially women. It goes against our instincts to build relationships and truly listen. So, how do we change the narrative?

What is a Pitch Without the Slap?

A pitch without the slap is a conversation with purpose. It's about making a genuine connection, understanding who you're speaking to, and creating a two-way exchange. It starts with curiosity about the other person—their needs, goals, and challenges. Instead of leading with what you have to sell, you lead with who you are, what you believe, and how you can help.

When you're pitching, it's not just about what you say—it's about how well you're reading the room. Paying attention to the other person's body language and energy can give you invaluable clues as to whether your message is landing or if you need to pivot.

Are they leaning in with interest, nodding, and asking follow-up questions? Those are signs you're on target, and the connection is building. On the other hand, if they're glancing away, folding their arms, or looking distracted, it's a signal that you may be losing them. These subtle cues help you course-correct in real time, adjusting your approach to keep the conversation engaging.

Turn Your Story Into Business Gold

The goal is to always stay tuned in to how the other person is reacting. If you notice disinterest, it's a chance to pause and ask a question, reframe your pitch, or bring the focus back to them. Reading the room effectively allows you to steer the conversation based on their level of engagement, which can make or break the success of your pitch.

This flips the whole "pitch slap" on its head. Instead of pushing a product or service, you're offering a solution that aligns with the other person's values and desires. It's less about "How can I sell you this?" and more about "How can I help you?" That simple shift in mindset makes all the difference.

A good pitch should feel like a natural part of the conversation, not a sales ambush. It's about offering value and showing how you can solve a problem or improve their situation—whether through your product, service, or expertise. This kind of pitch builds trust, engages the other person, and makes them feel heard.

> *A good pitch is natural. It's about "How can I help you?"*

When you craft your story, you're not just telling people what you do—you're differentiating yourself in a way that eliminates competition. By narrowing in on the specific aspects of your story and expertise, you stop being 'one of many' and become the go-to person in a unique niche. It's no longer about competing in a crowded field; it's about positioning yourself as the only solution for a particular audience.

For example, I helped Kim identify her strengths, which allowed her to move from being one of many life coaches

Chapter 3: Escaping the Pitch Trap

to becoming a mindset expert with a focus on wealth-building for chiropractors. It wasn't just about getting more specific—it was about making her stand out as *the* expert in that niche. The more refined and unique your story becomes, the less competition you have because you now position yourself as the specialist people seek out.

By doing this, you're no longer competing with everyone—you're becoming the obvious choice for clients who need exactly what you offer.

A pitch isn't about closing the deal on the spot. It's about opening the door, creating a relationship, and laying the groundwork for future partnerships. You're planting seeds, not rushing to harvest them.

Redefining the Pitch: From Sales to Connection

The key to escaping the pitch slap trap is building real relationships by asking thoughtful questions and showing genuine interest. When you do this, the "ask" feels less like a sale and more like a mutual decision.

Let's stop thinking of pitching as a sales tactic. Instead, see it as an opportunity to connect, listen, and serve. Every conversation is a chance to build trust, and trust is what leads to long-term success.

Imagine a conversation with a potential client. Instead of jumping straight into your pitch, start by asking: What challenges are they facing? What are their goals? How can you help—even if it's not about selling them something right away? When you focus on them rather than closing the deal, the conversation flows naturally, and often, the sale follows.

One of my clients made this shift from selling to connecting. Instead of pitching right out of the gate, she asked her clients about their goals, what they loved about their business, and how she could support them. Not only did this build loyalty, but it also boosted her sales. Why? Because people trusted her. She wasn't just focused on closing a deal—she was genuinely interested in them.

Shifting Your Mindset

We'll dive deeper into using stories to ease the awkwardness of sales in a later chapter, but right now, let's talk about mindset when it comes to pitching. I know you're probably thinking, "Oh no, not mindset!" But hear me out: success in business (and life) is 90% mindset. The way we approach pitching mentally can make or break the experience. Now that we've redefined what a pitch should be, it's time to shift how we think about it.

Much of the tension around pitching comes from old habits and fears—scarcity, rejection, and perfectionism. These mindset traps hold us back from making real connections.

Let's explore three key mindset shifts that will help you move beyond the pitch slap and embrace a more human approach:

Chapter 3: Escaping the Pitch Trap

1. From Scarcity to Abundance

Pitching from a place of scarcity is like operating with blinders on. You're so focused on closing the deal that you lose sight of the bigger picture—the relationship, the connection, and the potential for future opportunities. The scarcity mindset says, "I have to make this sale right now, or I'll miss out."

But what if you flipped that thinking? An abundance mindset says, "Opportunities are everywhere. I don't need to rush or force anything." When you trust that building relationships will naturally lead to opportunities down the road, it takes the pressure off both you and the person you're pitching to. Instead of scrambling for the sale, you focus on creating a genuine connection.

I worked with a massage therapist who was building her online business. She wanted to increase leads and simplify her marketing, but she hesitated over the cost. Instead of pushing for the sale, I asked her, "If money weren't an issue, what else would hold you back?" That one question shifted the conversation from scarcity—focusing on the price—to abundance—exploring her deeper concerns. She realized she needed to feel confident in the value of the investment. Once we found a plan that fit her budget, she felt empowered to move forward.

By addressing her deeper concerns instead of rushing to close the deal, the sale became the natural next step. When you operate from an abundance mindset, you're not racing to secure the deal—you're offering value, building trust, and knowing that the right opportunities will follow.

2. From Rejection to Curiosity

The fear of rejection is powerful. It makes us pitch too soon, push too hard, and talk way too much. When you're afraid of hearing "no," you instinctively try to control the conversation, which ends up feeling forced and uncomfortable for everyone.

But what if you shifted your mindset from fear to curiosity? Instead of worrying about rejection, approach the conversation with genuine interest. What are their goals? What challenges do they face? How can you serve them—even if they don't buy from you today? By focusing on curiosity, you become a better listener, and rejection stings less because you're now focused on learning and understanding, not just selling.

I worked with a female entrepreneur who struggled with this exact issue. She hated pitching because she didn't want people to feel pressured, and a "no" felt personal—like they were rejecting **her**, not just her services. This mindset was holding her back from building deeper relationships. She wanted to be seen as a trusted guide, but anything that felt like imposing made her uncomfortable.

When we reframed her approach to lead with curiosity and empathy—focusing on connection instead of closing—her sales skyrocketed. She wasn't "pitching" anymore; she was building trust. The more she listened and empathized, the more clients came to her because they felt heard and understood.

Chapter 3: Escaping the Pitch Trap

3. From Perfectionism to Authenticity

We often feel pressure to deliver the "perfect" pitch—polished, rehearsed, flawless. But here's the truth: perfection creates distance. When your pitch is too robotic or overly rehearsed, it becomes harder for people to connect with you.

The solution? Ditch perfectionism and embrace authenticity. Be human in your pitch. Share stories, be vulnerable, and let the conversation flow naturally. People don't connect with perfection—they connect with authenticity. When you show up as your real self, imperfections and all, your pitch feels genuine, and people are far more likely to trust and engage with you.

I remember a business owner whose pitch was so polished it sounded robotic. He rattled it off with precision, never smiled, and seemed relieved when it was over, so he could finally have a "real" conversation. His perfectionism created a barrier between him and his audience.

The more you practice these mindset shifts, the more natural and authentic your pitches will become—and the less you'll feel the need to "pitch" at all.

Shifting the Purpose of Your Pitch

Asking for the sale with confidence is just one part of the equation. But what if we completely reframe what pitching actually means? A pitch isn't a scripted monologue or a high-pressure tactic. At its core, pitching should be a conversation—an opportunity to connect, listen, and discover if there's a true fit between you and the other person. It's about creating space for collaboration, not forcing someone into a decision.

When you approach a pitch solely to land the sale, you create an atmosphere of pressure—both for yourself and the person you're speaking to. The focus shifts to what you want, not what they need. And that's where most pitches go wrong.

At one point, I had four different people pitch me collagen within a single week. Not one of them asked if I was already using it or even if I was interested in its benefits. Had they asked one simple question, it could've led to a completely different conversation. Instead, they were so focused on pushing their product that they missed the chance to connect with me.

Imagine if they had started with, "Are you currently using collagen?" or "What are you looking for in a supplement?" That shift would have shown genuine interest in my needs instead of pushing a one-size-fits-all pitch. But instead? I tuned them out.

This is why leading with curiosity and empathy matters. When you begin by understanding where your clients are and what they need, you create space for a real conversation. Instead of making them feel like a sales target, you make them feel heard—and that's where the magic happens.

The key is to let go of the need for a specific outcome and instead, invite a conversation to explore whether there's a real fit. When you focus on that, the pressure disappears, and the other person feels respected. They're no longer a target; they become part of the solution. When you give them the choice of whether working together is right, they feel far more invested and excited.

I recently worked with a business that completely transformed its approach by adopting this invitation-based method. Instead of diving straight into a pitch, they invited potential clients to a discovery conversation—an open dialogue to explore whether their services were a good match. There was no rush or urgency to "seal the deal." It was simply about finding genuine value. The results? Clients felt more engaged, empowered, and excited to move forward. They weren't being pushed; they were being invited to collaborate.

This approach shifts the dynamic from "I need to sell you something" to "Let's explore how we can solve this together." When you pitch this way, it feels more like a partnership. You're not pushing someone to take action—you're guiding them to a decision they feel confident about making.

By letting go of the traditional idea of pitching and turning it into a collaborative conversation, the tone changes completely. It becomes more genuine, human, and far less transactional. You're not trying to convince someone to work with you—you're offering them the opportunity to choose you. When people feel empowered to make that choice, they're more likely to move forward with confidence because they own the decision.

Even if someone doesn't choose to work with you right away, this approach leaves a positive impression. You've shown respect for their needs and demonstrated that your focus is on creating real value, not just closing a deal. That kind of integrity builds long-term trust. And even if they don't say "yes" today, they might refer you to others or come back when the timing is right.

By shifting the purpose of your pitch from closing a deal to creating a meaningful dialogue, you open the door to deeper relationships, greater trust, and more lasting success.

Conclusion:

At the heart of it, pitching isn't about pushing a product or begging for a sale. It's about stepping fully into your power, owning the value you bring, and creating genuine connections with the people you're meant to serve. When you lead with empathy, confidence, and a true commitment to adding value, you're not just another voice in a crowded marketplace—you're a force to be reckoned with.

Stop thinking of pitching as a hurdle to overcome. Instead, see it as an invitation—an opportunity to explore how your expertise can transform someone else's world. When you show up authentically and own your worth, the right clients are naturally drawn to what you offer. There's no need to chase or convince because the connection you build does the heavy lifting for you.

Here's the thing: your story, your expertise, and your solutions are enough. You don't need a perfect script or a rehearsed pitch. You need to trust that what makes you

Chapter 3: Escaping the Pitch Trap

unique is more powerful than any hard sell ever could be. You're not here to just close deals—you're here to create meaningful, lasting relationships with people who will benefit from what you offer.

So, let go of the pressure to perform. Lean into what makes you real. Build the kind of trust that isn't transactional, but transformational. That's how you move from simply selling to making a real impact.

And remember—when you focus on connection over conversion, you don't just build clients; you build **champions** for your business. People who trust you, who will refer you, and who will come back to you time and time again because they know you've got their back.

In the next chapter, we'll dive into how to craft a pitch that brings all of this to life—a pitch that's upgraded, snazzy, and grounded in everything we've covered here.

Key Takeaways

1. **Lead with Empathy and Value** – When you focus on truly understanding your client's needs and offering real value, the pitch naturally follows. Empathy opens the door to trust.

2. **Reframe Your Pitch** – See pitching as a collaborative conversation. It's about you and your client exploring together whether your services align with their needs.

3. **Focus on Connection, Not Pressure** – Shift from a transactional mindset to one of curiosity and connection. When clients feel heard and understood, they're more open to working with you.

4. **Pitch as a Partnership** – Approach pitching as a partnership, where you and your client work together to find the right solution. It's about collaboration, not persuasion.

Mindset Shifts:

1. **From Transactional to Relational** – Shift your mindset from seeing pitching as a transaction to viewing it as an opportunity to connect and collaborate with potential clients.

2. **From Selling to Solving** – Focus on solving your client's problem rather than simply selling your product. This approach makes your pitch more authentic and client-centered.

3. **Embrace "No" as Valuable Feedback** – Every "no" is an opportunity to refine your approach and find the right fit for your business.

Action Steps:

1. **Review Your Pitch for Empathy** – Look at a recent pitch. Did you jump straight to the offer? Rewrite it to emphasize problem-solving and relationship-building.

Chapter 3: Escaping the Pitch Trap

2. **Shift to Invitation-Based Pitching** – In your next pitch, invite the client to explore whether working together is a good fit, rather than pressuring them to buy immediately. Focus on creating a partnership.

3. **Listen More Than You Speak** – In your next conversation, make a conscious effort to listen more than you talk. Pay attention to their needs and goals, and reflect on how you can offer value.

4. **Evaluate Other Pitches** – Pay attention to how others pitch to you—whether in person, online, or through email. What resonates with you, and what feels off? Consider how you can apply those insights to your own pitch.

If you haven't yet gotten your complimentary companion Workbook to go deeper and actually write our your thoughts, shifts, and steps, scan the code to get it now:

Chapter 4
Crafting a Winning Pitch

" Purpose isn't found in the grand narratives—it's discovered in the stories we tell every day, where even the smallest moment can ignite the biggest change." –
Leslie Capps, Wild Woman Marketing

Storytelling is more than a feel-good connection tool; it's a strategic asset that transforms how you engage with your audience. In business, stories aren't just for entertainment—they're crafted to inspire action, build trust, and guide your audience toward taking the next step with you.

The real power of storytelling lies in its ability to open doors, spark curiosity, and shift perspectives. Whether you're pitching an idea, crafting marketing messages, or talking with potential clients, it's not enough for your story to simply entertain. It has to do the heavy lifting—it's gotta move people toward making a decision. When used strategically, storytelling becomes the ultimate door opener.

But here's the thing: not all stories are created equal. To craft a pitch that sticks, your story needs to hit the right notes at the right time for the right people. It pulls people into your world, piques their curiosity, and makes them lean in, thinking, "Okay, now you've got my attention." This is where the magic happens—when people feel something, they start trusting you. And trust? That's the foundation of every great relationship, in business and beyond.

Think about networking. Everyone expects to get pitched, right? But when you lead with a story instead of diving into a sales spiel, you change the entire dynamic. Suddenly, instead of thinking, "Here comes another pitch," they're leaning in, intrigued, saying, "Okay, this is different. Tell me more." That's the power of a great story—it opens the door without you even needing to knock.

> *The right story builds connection and opens the door of opportunity.*

And here's the truth: we're all looking for solutions. At the end of the day, we spend our hard-earned money with people we know, like, and trust—the holy trinity of business success. And storytelling? It's your golden ticket to building that trifecta and creating an audience of raving fans who will buy from you, cheer for you, and spread the word about you.

How do you make this happen in your pitch? It's simple—start with the problem your audience needs solved. Weave your story as the bridge from "I understand your problem" to "I might have the solution." Your story isn't just a way to share your message—it's the road map that leads your audience straight to the solution they've been searching for.

Pitching with a Story-First Mindset

The best way to start a pitch is by engaging your audience emotionally. Lead them into understanding why they need your offer through a story. Take Robin, for example. Her story centered around taking control of her health when traditional medicine let her down. She discovered how to support her body's natural healing process. Originally, her pitch bogged down in the 'how,' overwhelming listeners with the technicalities of a liver cleanse—not the sexiest of topics.

So, we flipped her strategy and her script. Instead of overwhelming people with the process, we led with her why: 'I'm known as the Queen of Healthy Living because I've helped 254 women transform their health and live longer, better lives with simple recipes.' This shift in her pitch pulled people in, showing them how her approach benefited their lives without getting lost in unnecessary details.

A great story elevates your message, making it engaging and relatable, whether you're pitching, writing a social post, or speaking at an event. Humor is a great way to cut through the noise, but it has to bridge the gap between the joke and your message. Just because you find something funny doesn't mean your audience will see the connection.

I recall sitting through a presentation on key performance indicators where the speaker used an acronym—AARGH, like a pirate. My brain got stuck on the pirate imagery, and I completely missed the point. He wasn't just off-mark for me; about 80% of the attendees felt lost. His attempt at creativity didn't open any doors—it left us all wondering what he was trying to sell. Stories only work if they align with your audience's expectations and needs.

Your story needs to match your message and connect with what your audience wants. Let's dive into how you can craft a pitch that truly grabs attention.

Structuring Your Story-Driven Pitch

When it comes to pitching, time is your nemesis. In a 30- to 60-second pitch, you don't have the luxury of telling a full, detailed story. Instead, your job is to pull out the most compelling parts—the pieces that grab attention and speak directly to your audience's needs. It's not about telling a full, chronological story; it's about using the right fragments to spark curiosity, establish a connection, and show why your solution matters.

This is about tapping into what makes you special. Saying, "I'm a life coach," doesn't set you apart, and you can lose people with the first few words. Whatever broad label you use, there are a gazillion people doing the same thing. If you're still with me, I'm 90% sure you've got a fabulous product or service that the world needs.

Here's the question: why would someone buy from you versus Joe, the guy next door? Lean into this challenge—

this is where you need to be truthful about what you do that is freaking amazing.

How do we structure this beast? For a pitch to resonate, you need to extract the elements that highlight why your solution matters, what makes it different, and what is the special sauce that you bring to the table. A condensed narrative need not sacrifice depth—it means distilling your message down to the most essential, emotionally compelling elements.

When crafting a story-driven pitch, each part should work together to guide your audience from curiosity to action. It's not just about telling a story—it's about strategically building a connection that highlights why your solution is the answer they've been looking for. Here's how to break it down step by step:

1. **The Hook**: (the Beginning)

   Start with a compelling, relatable problem or challenge that your audience can identify with. Creating a unique label that sums up what you do in just a few words helps make an immediate impression and gets them listening.

   "I'm known as the strategic storyteller because if you give me five minutes, I can pull out the story that's hidden in you—the story your audience wants and needs to hear so they buy your product or service."

   Avoid overused phrases like *"What if I told you..."* or *"Let me tell you a story."* No, please don't. Your audience already knows a pitch is coming, so skip the buildup and dive right into the issue.

Instead, opt for something that feels natural and engaging. *"Maybe you've never struggled to get leads, but I sure have, and it was miserable, and that's why....";* *"Did you know 80% of online business owners won't make it past the second year?"*

2. **The Journey**: (the Middle)

   Now, share an experience that directly relates to your audience's problem. The journey doesn't need to be grand; it just needs to be relevant and relatable to your audience without getting lost in the details.

   "I helped a business owner reframe his introductory pitch, and after making a few tweaks, he signed two new clients within 24 hours."

3. **The Solution**: (the End)

   Present your product, service, or idea as the natural solution to the problem. Your story should flow right into this without feeling forced.

   "My mission is to change the 80/20 rule so that 80% of entrepreneurs use their stories to attract more clients and elevate their brand."

4. **The Bridge**: (the Lesson)

   Here's where you explain why this story matters. This is the personal or insightful takeaway that ties everything

Chapter 4: Crafting a Winning Pitch

together. It answers the question, *"Why am I telling you this?"*

" I spent thousands of dollars looking for a better marketing and sales system. Who knew the answer was getting clear on my messaging?"

5. **The Call To Action**: (the Invitation)

   End with a clear, direct call to action. Invite your audience to take the next step with you. It's not about closing a sale right away—it's about opening the door to more engagement, whether that's through a free resource, consultation, or community involvement.

   "If you want to refine your pitch and see instant results, take my free course."

The purpose of a story-driven pitch is to stand out and elevate your message beyond just another sales pitch. A pitch rooted in a story taps into emotions—and that's what people remember. Data points and facts don't stick in the same way. The emotional hook is key.

A marketing professional once told me a personal story about a traumatic injury and then jumped right into what he does for clients. I scratched my head and said, *"I don't see how these are related."* He casually replied, *"Oh, they're not."* If your story doesn't connect to your message, don't tell it. You have to connect the dots for your audience or the story falls flat.

Your story-driven pitch should be simple, clear, and provide breadcrumbs that lead directly to your solution, so the audience stays engaged. And if you use humor, make sure it lands with your specific audience—not just you. Humor that doesn't connect can be just as confusing as a story without a point.

Tailoring Your Story to Your Audience

The one-size-fits-all approach doesn't work for pitching. Think about it—just like you wouldn't wear the same outfit to every occasion, you shouldn't use the same story for every pitch. Your core story remains the same, but you can easily adjust the details and tone based on the audience—whether you're speaking to clients or collaborators.

For example, potential clients care about how you solve their immediate problem, while collaborators might be more interested in how your services complement theirs. By having a few key outcomes and pain points in mind, you can adjust your pitch on the fly.

Start by asking yourself: Who am I speaking to, and what do they need to hear? Even if you always speak to other entrepreneurs, you may be at a networking event that attracts speakers and podcast hosts. Then, consider what side of that equation you fall on and adjust accordingly.

I often introduce myself as "a strategic storyteller who helps uncover the hidden stories that resonate with audiences." When speaking to teachers about course creation, I shift the focus to say, "I help course creators develop stories that captivate their students." The

Chapter 4: Crafting a Winning Pitch

structure of the story doesn't change, but I've shifted the details to resonate with that specific audience. Here's a helpful networking trick: let the other person introduce themselves first. This gives you the chance to add or subtract elements of your story as needed. And here's a secret if you're in a group: rather than trying to generalize your message, speak to one. People tend to associate with like-minded folks, so keying in on one lets your story speak to many.

This is where emotional connection comes in. You don't need to rattle off all your credentials to make an impact. Instead, focus on what's relatable. I used to teach storytelling workshops using the Hero's Journey framework—it's a classic, but the more I worked with it, the more I realized it was overwhelming for people to grasp and apply. There were too many steps, too much theory, and by the time they tried to fit their story into it, they were exhausted and confused. I felt the same!

So, I simplified it. I stripped it down to the core elements that actually mattered to their business stories: the challenge, the solution, the lesson, and the action. The moment I made that shift, the workshop transformed. People engaged more, and they started seeing results because it was clear and actionable. I now use that same streamlined framework in my master storytelling workshops, and it works every time.

> *Tell the story that's relatable and builds relationship with your audience..*

It's not about overwhelming them with details; it's about zeroing in on the part of your story that makes them see themselves in you. When they can see themselves in your journey, they start to believe that your solution could be their solution, too.

Building Confidence in Your Pitch Delivery

Confidence is key when delivering your pitch. The more natural your story feels to tell, the more compelling it will be to your audience. The best way to build that confidence?

Practice.

Speed networking events are an excellent place to sharpen your pitch. You'll have multiple chances to deliver it in a short amount of time. Pay attention to how people respond to you and to others. What grabs your attention? What language and tone do you like? And what makes a pitch fall flat?

As you practice, you'll notice spots where things feel off—maybe there's a section where you stumble or a phrase that doesn't feel quite right. Those are the moments to tweak and refine. The more you practice, the smoother and more natural it will feel, and the more your confidence will grow.

Don't be afraid to ask for feedback—but skip the sugar coating. Cheerleaders are great, but you need honest input to really improve. Find mentors, coaches, or peers who will tell you the truth and help you refine your pitch.

Chapter 4: Crafting a Winning Pitch

And here's a secret: your pitch doesn't always have to be loud and bold. Sometimes, leaning in and lowering your voice can make all the difference. A whisper can pull people in just as much as raising your voice to emphasize a point. Play around with tone, body language, and delivery to see what feels most authentic for you.

As you continue refining your pitch, remember that outside feedback can bring new clarity. You might not always catch what needs improvement on your own, so a fresh perspective can help take your delivery to the next level.

Simplifying Your Story—Cutting Through the Weeds

Molly, a LinkedIn business coach, shared something that really struck me: *suffering is optional.*

Not everyone's story follows a dramatic arc, and it doesn't need to. Your story doesn't have to be about rock bottom to success. It just needs to resonate with you and feel authentic to your audience.

We can get hung up in thinking our story has to be dramatic to have impact. But sometimes, it's the small, seemingly insignificant moments that connect with people the most. Your story should cut through the noise and connect with your audience on a deeper level, without the unnecessary drama.

You've got to clear out your mental clutter. Whether you work with a coach or not, getting an outside perspective is key. As entrepreneurs, we've taken countless courses, invested tons of money, and have so much life experience, but when we're too close to our own story, it gets messy. We try to fit every experience into a thirty-second introduction.

When someone listens to your pitch, they'll help you pinpoint the parts of your story that resonate most with your audience. Not everything in your story is important right now—stick to the core. Your audience doesn't need the whole backstory upfront. Save those details for when they're already invested in you.

Closing the Pitch with a Story

Closing your pitch with a well-timed story is a powerful way to create a lasting emotional connection. Stories engage people on a level that facts and figures can't reach, leaving them with something to hold onto emotionally. When crafting your closing story, focus on tying it back to your core message and offering a final reminder of why your audience should care.

If you begin your pitch with a story, bring it full circle to reinforce your main message. If not, now's your chance to share a brief personal anecdote. Share a quick example of how your product or service changed someone's life or why you're passionate about what you do.

For example: *"I'll never forget the day one of my clients called me in tears, telling me how my product helped her get her energy back after years of struggling with fatigue. She went from barely getting through the day to running her first 5K. That's why I do what I do—to help people like her transform their lives."*

This final story doesn't just summarize your pitch—it drives home your message in a way that sticks with your audience long after the pitch ends.

The Value of Outside Feedback

As you shape your pitch, outside perspectives can make a world of difference. Sometimes, we're so close to our stories that we lose sight of how they're being received by others. This is where outside feedback—especially through networking—becomes invaluable, offering fresh eyes on your story and revealing blind spots you might not even realize exist.

Networking gives you a chance to test and adjust your message in real time. Here's a fun experiment: have five different introductions ready and attend a speed networking event. If possible, let the other person speak first, then choose the pitch that best aligns with them. Pay close attention to their reactions—are they leaning in, asking questions, or pulling away? This immediate feedback gives you insight into whether your story is hitting the mark.

You might find that one part of your story captures attention, but the next part makes the listener pull back. This could signal that the elements are there, but they need to be rearranged for greater impact. Feedback like this helps you improve not just the content but the flow of your message.

Networking isn't just about perfecting your own story. It's also about observing how others share themselves through their introduction. Take note of what grabs attention and what doesn't. Simply watching how people respond to different narratives can spark new ideas and offer a fresh perspective on your own messaging. This is a great way to see what resonates in real-world situations.

When you're networking, stay curious about the people you're talking to, especially if they're your ideal clients. Listen to the words they're using and the challenges they're facing. The more you understand their world, the better you can shape your message to speak directly to them.

Pay attention to the questions (or lack of them) that you're getting—if no one's asking, it might be a sign your story isn't connecting. On the flip side, engaging questions show interest and can help take the conversation deeper.

In this way, networking becomes more than just an exchange of business cards—it becomes a live testing ground. Every interaction is an opportunity to gather valuable feedback, adjust your story, and evolve your message while building meaningful relationships. The more you engage, the more clarity and confidence you'll gain in sharing your story.

Conclusion:

Your pitch isn't just about rattling off features or hoping something clicks. It's a story-driven strategy—a deliberate, crafted narrative that guides your audience through a

Chapter 4: Crafting a Winning Pitch

journey. It starts with a hook that draws them in, follows with a story that resonates and ends with a strong, unforgettable close. And here's the thing: when your story-driven pitch is done right, it doesn't just wrap up neatly—it leaves a lasting mark.

A compelling closing isn't just about tying everything together. It's about reminding your audience why you do what you do, and connecting that to why they need it. When you close with a story that resonates emotionally, you're not just offering a product or service—you're positioning yourself as the person who understands their needs and has the solution they're looking for. You've made it personal, not just about the sale.

That's the essence of the story-driven strategy. It's what sets you apart from others who are simply pitching for the sake of it. You're showing your audience that their story and yours are intertwined and that by working together, they can reach the outcomes they want.

Ask yourself: how does your close leave them feeling? Do they see the connection between their needs and your solution? Are they moved to take action, or will they forget your pitch the minute you walk out the door? When you finish with a strong, emotion-driven story, you're not just pitching—you're creating a memorable moment that inspires them to act.

That's the true power of a story-driven strategy—it's not just about selling. It's about leading your audience through a journey where the next logical step is working with you because they believe in both your story and theirs. When you close your pitch like that, you're not just leaving an impression. You're creating a relationship.

Key Takeaways

1. **Storytelling is Your Secret Weapon:** Crafting a story-driven pitch isn't just about entertaining your audience—it's a deliberate strategy that leads them toward a decision that benefits both of you. A well-told story doesn't just open doors; it connects on a deeper emotional level that sticks.

2. **One Pitch Doesn't Fit All:** A cookie-cutter pitch won't cut it. Tailor your story to the unique needs and pain points of your audience—whether they're clients, collaborators, or partners. Speak their language and make your story relevant to them.

3. **Emotion is What They Remember:** Forget the data dumps—people connect with stories. When you tap into the emotional core of your story, you create a bond that lasts beyond the pitch and makes you unforgettable.

4. **Leave Them with a Lasting Impression**: A strong pitch doesn't just end; it lingers. Closing with a powerful, emotionally charged story reinforces your message and leaves your audience with something to remember—and, more importantly, a reason to act.

Mindset Shifts:

1. **From Selling to Solving:** Shift your thinking from selling a product or service to solving a real problem for your audience. This makes your pitch feel more authentic and less transactional.

2. **Less is More:** Your story doesn't need to be elaborate or overly detailed to make an impact. Focus on the core, emotionally resonant elements that your audience can connect with.

3. **Confidence in Adaptability:** Understand that your story's core remains consistent, but the delivery can and should shift based on your audience. Embrace the flexibility of adapting your pitch to fit different situations without losing its essence.

Action Steps:

1. **Craft a Hook**: Write a short, two-sentence hook that introduces your story in a way that invites curiosity and engagement.

2. **Identify Key Journey Points:** Identify three key aspects of your journey that highlight the "why" behind what you do, not just the "how."

3. **Test Your Pitch:** Practice delivering your pitch to a trusted friend or colleague. Ask for feedback on how your story resonates emotionally. Does it connect with their pain points, or are there details that feel

unnecessary? Even better, take your new pitch and go networking.

4. **Record and Review:** Record yourself delivering the pitch. Does it flow naturally? Are you focusing too much on qualifications or data points rather than building an emotional connection?

If you haven't yet gotten your complimentary companion Workbook to go deeper and actually write our your thoughts, shifts, and steps, scan the code to get it now:

Chapter 5
Storytelling as the Ultimate Business Tool

"Strategically using my story built a business of empowerment, helping women transform pain into confidence and embrace unshakeable inner strength with authenticity."
– Dharma Rebecca Funder, Spiritual Dynamics Consortium

Storytelling isn't just a nice-to-have in business—it's the foundation of how we connect, lead, and grow. It's like the Swiss Army knife in your business toolkit: multi-purpose, essential, and often underestimated until you start using it. Whether you're leading a team, building relationships with clients, or breaking down complex ideas, storytelling makes everything clearer and more powerful.

In today's market, where everyone's drowning in options and information, it's your story that sets you apart. It's not about getting eyes on you; it's about making real connections. It goes deeper than the products or services you sell—it's about who you are, what you stand for, and how that resonates with your audience. That's the magic of strategic storytelling—it creates trust and builds relationships in ways numbers and features never will.

Your brand? It's more than a logo, a clever tagline, or a pretty color palette. Sure, those catch attention, but they don't create emotional connections that stick. What makes your brand memorable? It's the story behind it—your mission, your values, and most importantly, your "why."

Think about the brands you're loyal to. It wasn't just the product or service that hooked you—it was the feeling their story gave you. It's how they show up and what they stand for. Your brand's story does the same thing. It doesn't just tell people what you do; it tells them why you do it and how you got here.

Here's the thing: Entrepreneurs often think that the right tagline or sleek logo is enough to make their brand unforgettable. Sure, those things help with your visuals, but they're not the foundation. Your brand's identity isn't built on what you do—it's shaped by the stories that bring it to life. That's why storytelling is your secret weapon—it communicates your values and "why" like nothing else can.

The Human Side of Branding

As entrepreneurs, we are our brand. It's our personal experiences, challenges, and victories that make us

Chapter 5: Storytelling as the Ultimate Business Tool

relatable. Sharing real moments through storytelling gives people a reason to connect with you—not just your product or service. Your story shows what you stand for, what you value, and what people can expect when they work with you.

Storytelling isn't just about your big wins or polished success. It's the stumbles, the messes, and those times you had to figure things out on the fly that really hit home. Those moments make you human. When your audience sees that, assurance and connection follow naturally. That's the power of storytelling—taking your brand from functional to unforgettable.

As a single entrepreneur, your personal story and your brand story often overlap. Your personal journey—the challenges, insights, and experiences that shaped who you are—often becomes part of your brand's identity. Your brand story, however, is more outward-facing—it's the message you want your audience to connect with, rooted in your mission and the impact your business has. While your personal story is about you, the brand story is about what your business offers and the change it creates for others.

> *Your audience wants to know who you are and will connect with your humanity in your story.*

Crafting a brand story isn't about rigid formulas, but there are key elements that make it powerful. Your brand story should reflect your mission—why your business exists and what problem you're solving. It should also highlight your values—what you stand for and how those values show up in your work.

Finally, it's about impact—the change you aim to create for your customers or the world. When these elements come together, your brand story becomes more than just a narrative; it becomes a clear expression of what your business is all about and why it matters.

As an entrepreneur, there's often a blend between your personal brand and your company brand. Understanding how to distinguish and balance these two is key.

Personal Brand vs. Company Brand

Your personal brand reflects who you are—the experiences, values, and personality that make you unique as a leader. Your company brand, on the other hand, is the collective identity of your business—its mission, values, and story. As a single entrepreneur, these often overlap. But here's the thing: your personal story is about you, while your brand story is about the impact your business creates for others.

Take Sara Blakely, the founder of Spanx. Her personal story—starting with $5,000 and a dream—has become a key part of the Spanx brand identity. While Spanx's brand focuses on creating innovative, comfortable undergarments, Blakely's story of perseverance and entrepreneurial grit makes the company relatable and inspiring to customers and employees alike. That's a good brand story—it connects a personal mission with a company mission, building loyalty and credibility.

Now, let's consider what makes a bad brand story. A brand story that doesn't resonate or feels disconnected from its

Chapter 5: Storytelling as the Ultimate Business Tool

audience can fall flat. For example, a tech company that highlights how innovative and complex its products are but doesn't show how those products solve real-world problems, fails to build a connection. It might sound impressive on the surface, but without an emotional hook, the audience doesn't engage. In this case, the story is all about features and none of the heart.

That's why it's so important to recognize: whether or not you actively acknowledge it, you have a brand. Every business has a story that's either working for or against them. The key is to own it, refine it, and make sure it's a story worth telling.

The Hub of Your Marketing

Once your brand's story is grounded in your values, mission, and experiences, it becomes easier to integrate storytelling into your marketing. Instead of relying on traditional marketing tactics, which can feel impersonal, storytelling allows you to engage your audience on a deeper, more authentic level. You're not just selling a product or service—you're sharing real experiences that resonate with your audience on a personal level.

Take for example, the virtual assistant agency I worked with that offered over 300 services. Impressive, but overwhelming for potential clients. Instead of listing features, we reframed their narrative to say, "We lighten the load for business owners, so they can focus on what matters most." This simple messaging shift cut through the noise of their overloaded services list and created a stronger emotional connection with their clients.

When you build your marketing around storytelling, you're doing more than promoting a product—you're showing your audience how you can help solve their problems and create meaningful transformations.

For instance, a tech client was struggling with jargon-heavy messaging that wasn't resonating with their audience. We flipped the focus to the impact they made: "We help companies protect their data, so they can focus on innovation without worrying about cybersecurity threats." Instantly, the value became clear—no complex technical details needed.

At the heart of marketing is relationship-building. When you center your marketing strategy on storytelling, your content moves beyond just sharing information—it taps into emotions. That's how you create a brand people want to engage with, talk about, and recommend. When your audience sees themselves in your story, connect with you, and keep coming back.

The Lever in Your Leadership

In leadership, stories aren't just tools—they inspire action. A leader who knows how to tell a great story doesn't just set goals or give instructions; they take their team on a journey. It's about showing your team that you've been through challenges but come out stronger, and they can, too.

People don't connect with titles—they connect with the person behind them. When leaders share stories of growth, tough lessons, and even failures, they build trust.

Chapter 5: Storytelling as the Ultimate Business Tool

That kind of transparency? It creates loyalty. And loyalty? That's what drives action. No one follows perfection; they follow the real person who shows up behind the title.

True leadership isn't just about handing out tasks; it's about guiding people through the ups and downs with empathy and strength. When your stories reflect your values, it invites others to join you on the ride. A good story helps your team see they're being led by someone who truly gets it.

> *No one follows perfection. True leadership storytelling invites others in to create the bigger picture through the challenges.*

Leadership storytelling isn't about boasting wins—it's about sharing the messy, real moments when you overcame challenges and giving your team a way to see themselves in that journey. The secret to getting your team engaged isn't broadcasting your success—it's showing them your vulnerability and keeping it real.

Look at Howard Schultz when he returned to Starbucks during a rough patch. Instead of just diving into business strategies, he reminded the team of the company's original mission: to be a community hub for customers. His personal story brought everyone back to the heart of the company, and it helped turn things around.

Sharing your struggles sends a clear message: it's okay to fail, as long as you learn and keep moving forward. People connect to those kinds of stories because they're real. Perfection? It's not relatable. Real life is messy, and that's what your team faces every day. Your job is to keep it human, not ideal.

To keep your team fired up, drop in a story when the energy's low or share a win when things are tight on deadlines. A perfectly timed story can shift the vibe and refocus everyone on the bigger picture.

Still finding your storytelling groove? Don't sweat it—it's a process. Start by learning from the leaders you admire and let their stories inspire you until your own voice starts shining through. Leadership grows with every story you tell, one step at a time.

Telling Stories That Lead

Look, being a leader is more than just calling the shots. It's about building real, human connections. And the secret weapon? You guessed it: storytelling. But not just any story—you need relatable stories that make people sit up and say, "Oh yeah, I've been there." Here's how to share those stories in a way that'll have your team rallying behind you.

1. **Pick Stories That Hit Home**

    Don't dig out that one perfect win from five years ago if it doesn't fit the moment. Look for the times you faced the same grind your team is going through right now.

    If your team's burning the midnight oil, share the time you pulled an all-nighter to make magic

Chapter 5: Storytelling as the Ultimate Business Tool

happen and how it paid off. They'll see you've been in the trenches, too—that's where respect is built.

2. **Ditch the Perfection—Keep it Real**

   Perfection is boring, improbable, and definitely not relatable. Share your struggles, your messy moments, and how you bounced back. People love a good comeback story. That's what they connect with, and it's what makes you human.

3. **Remember Your 'Why'**

   Why are you sharing the story? Every story needs a clear message—something that sticks. Think about what you want your team to walk away with. Is it resilience? Creativity? A reminder that they can handle whatever's coming their way?

   If teamwork is falling flat, don't just throw out a "let's work together" speech. Tell them about a time when collaboration saved the day—and how working together can move mountains.

4. **Get Them Talking**

   It's not all about you. Ask your team to share their stories. People connect faster when they feel heard. So after you drop your story, open the floor for them to chime in. It builds confidence and shows that you care about their journey, too.

Creating a Shared Vision Through Stories

In business, storytelling isn't just a way to communicate goals—it's a way to share the deeper values and motivations behind them. A well-told story helps people see the bigger picture and feel emotionally invested in the outcome.

Take a woman leading a nonprofit for homeless youth. She might share her personal story of growing up in poverty and how it shaped her commitment to the cause. By intertwining her personal experience with the organization's mission, she doesn't just gain donors—she creates a shared sense of purpose that energizes volunteers, staff, and the broader community. Her story turns the nonprofit into more than just a service provider—it becomes a movement fueled by personal connection.

Similarly, the CEO of Patagonia regularly shares stories about the company's commitment to environmental sustainability. By telling stories of how their efforts have led to real-world environmental changes, the team feels more connected to the mission. It's not just about selling products—it's about protecting the planet. This shared sense of purpose fuels employees' passion and turns them into advocates for the brand's vision.

Storytelling doesn't just align your team with a shared vision—it builds something much larger. When your story resonates deeply with your audience, it can grow into a thriving community united by shared values and goals. That connection is what transforms a business or organization from a service provider into a hub where people find belonging, purpose, and support.

Building a Community Through Storytelling

Storytelling doesn't just inspire—it builds communities united by shared values and goals. Take Victoria, for example. She turned her passion for wellness into a thriving community by sharing her personal health journey on social media. Her openness attracted a following of like-minded individuals who connected with her story on a personal level.

After sharing her struggles with health and wellness, Victoria saw her story take on a life of its own. Her followers didn't just buy her wellness products—they became part of a larger conversation. She hosted online challenges and shared client stories, which encouraged others to share their own. Soon, it wasn't just her journey—it was a community of people supporting each other. This storytelling-driven community led to more than just sales—it became a place where people felt understood and supported. Together, they built something bigger than any one of them could have imagined.

The power of storytelling in building communities isn't just about your story—it's about inviting others to share theirs. Leaders who foster community go beyond simply telling their journey; they make room for others to contribute. Collective storytelling strengthens communities, turning followers into a tribe united by shared experiences.

Encouraging people to open up creates a space where everyone feels they belong. Instead of positioning yourself as the sole storyteller, you empower your community to contribute. By making space for clients, customers, or team members to share their experiences, you turn storytelling into a two-way street. The stories of others become woven into the fabric of your brand or mission, creating a sense of shared ownership in the community.

The Core of Your Client Relationships

Storytelling is one of the most powerful ways to build credibility with clients. People connect with personal stories far more than with dry facts or product information. Stories engage the emotional part of the brain, which is why they stick. In client relationships, this is crucial because clients aren't just looking for a solution; they're looking for someone to guide them. A well-told story turns promises into proof that you've been there before and helped others succeed.

> *Effective storytelling is about building community and making room for others to share their stories too.*

Take a friend of mine who recently hired a contractor for a bathroom remodel. She didn't go with the lowest bid; she went with the contractor who listened to her vision and shared how he'd helped other clients bring similar projects to life. The contractor didn't just sell a service—he addressed her concerns and crafted solutions that blended the practical with her dream bathroom vision.

Storytelling works so well in client relationships because it's more than just a transaction. When you share a story, your clients see themselves in it. They can picture themselves overcoming challenges, hitting their goals, and finding success—because they've seen how it played out for someone else. That emotional connection? That's what makes stories stick.

And hey, even if you're just starting out and don't have many client success stories yet, that's no problem. You've still got a story worth telling. Focus on your "why"—why you started this business in the first place, the experiences that shaped your mission, and the vision you have for your clients. People buy into your passion and purpose just as much as your services. Trust is built on authenticity, and your journey is enough to do that, even without a long list of case studies.

How to Use Client Stories Effectively

Once you've worked with clients, start sharing their success stories. But here's the thing—don't just list their wins. Bring their journey to life. How did they feel when they first came to you? What challenges were they up against? And how did your service or solution help turn things around for them? These stories do more than just promote your business—they build trust. When potential clients hear about someone with similar struggles who made it through with your help, they start seeing themselves in that same success.

Example: Let's say you're a business coach, and your client, Jane, came to you feeling overwhelmed and stuck in her business. Over a few months, you helped her refocus her strategy, streamline operations, and double her revenue. But don't just rattle off those results—tell the story of Jane's transformation. Talk about how she felt when she started, what her turning point was, and how she felt after that big

Turn Your Story Into Business Gold

win. This makes the story relatable and emotional, creating a deeper connection with your audience.

In business, credibility is everything. Clients don't want to feel pushed toward a transaction—they want to feel understood. When you share stories that highlight how you've helped others solve problems and achieve results, you're building something deeper than a transaction—you're showing that you understand their needs and have a track record of delivering.

Client stories are powerful because they help reassure potential clients that they're making the right decision by choosing you. When they hear about others who were in their shoes and succeeded, it strengthens their confidence in you and in the solutions you offer. Instead of focusing on the sale, focus on authentic connections—this is what builds lasting relationships and turns first-time clients into long-term partners.

Asking for Client Stories

Don't hesitate to ask clients for feedback after you've worked with them. It's a simple request, but it leads to powerful insights you may not have seen coming. Often, what clients value most isn't always what you expect. Maybe you thought your strategic advice was the game-changer, but your client found your steady support and encouragement to be the real standout. These insights are goldmines for future storytelling, helping you sharpen your message and connect more deeply with new clients.

Start weaving these client stories into your conversations, presentations, or marketing. When potential clients hear real-world success stories, they're not just hearing about what you offer—they're seeing what's possible for them.

Conclusion

Storytelling isn't just another tool in your business—it's the backbone of everything you do. Leading with stories is more than offering a product or service; it involves building real, lasting relationships based on confidence and understanding. Your story helps people connect with you as someone who truly gets what they're going through and knows how to help them move forward.
In today's crowded marketplace, traditional sales and marketing can feel distant and impersonal. Storytelling flips the script. It lets you build credibility through shared experiences and relatable stories, helping your audience picture themselves in the solutions you offer. This makes your business not just a choice, but the partner they trust to help them succeed.

What sets you apart isn't just the technical stuff—it's the unique stories that show your purpose, values, and vision. When you weave your story into everything you do—from sales to leadership to client relationships—you create real connections that stick long after that first conversation.

Now's the time to take action. Start using storytelling in every corner of your business. Whether you're sharing a story with a client or leading your team, your story can shape the relationships you build and the impact you make.

Turn Your Story Into Business Gold

Your audience is ready to connect—tell your story and let it do the work.

Key Takeaways

1. **Storytelling as the foundation**: It's not just a marketing tactic—it's the backbone of how you connect, lead, and build credibility. Stories build deeper relationships by communicating your purpose, values, and vision.

2. **Stories build connections**: Stories help your audience see themselves in the solutions you offer, making your business the preferred partner.

3. **Tailor your story**: Whether in sales, leadership, or client relationships, the best stories resonate because they're relatable and purposeful. Be clear on the goal of your story and shape it to meet your audience's needs.

4. **Take action with storytelling**: Start using storytelling in every part of your business, from sales conversations to team leadership. Your story is a powerful tool for building trust, inspiring action, and making a lasting impact.

Mindset Shifts:

1. **From Selling to Storytelling:** Shift toward storytelling as a natural way to engage, inspire, and

build relationships. The goal isn't just to sell—it's to connect.

2. **From Facts to Emotions**: Move away from information-heavy conversations and focus on creating emotionally engaging experiences.

3. **From You to Them:** Focus on how your story clicks with your audience. It's about showing them how they fit into the solution, not just telling them about your wins.

Action Steps

1. **Identify Your Core Stories**: Pinpoint key stories from your personal and professional journey that highlight your mission, values, and the impact you've made. These stories should resonate with your audience and reflect the challenges you've overcome.

2. **Incorporate Stories into Team Leadership**: Share stories with your team that illustrate leadership through challenges, resilience, or growth. Use these stories to inspire your team and align them with your mission and goals.

3. **Integrate Storytelling in Client Conversations**: The next time you meet with a potential client, use a relevant story to show how you've helped others overcome similar challenges. Focus on creating an emotional connection instead of just presenting services.

4. **Ask for Client Stories**: After finishing a project or engagement, ask your clients for feedback on what stood out to them. Use these insights to create new stories that highlight your impact and build loyalty with future clients.

If you haven't yet gotten your complimentary companion Workbook to go deeper and actually write our your thoughts, shifts, and steps, scan the code to get it now:

Chapter 6
Evolving Your Story as You Grow

"One day, one moment, one breath at a time, you will build up the courage to overcome."
– Christina Sommers, Breath of Renewal

Every entrepreneur's journey is a series of evolving stories. Just like a book, your story unfolds in chapters—you don't need to retell every detail every time you speak. Instead, focus on the chapters that matter most in the moment, the ones that align with where you are in your business and who you're speaking to right now.

Stepping into a bigger version of yourself isn't about erasing your past; it's about amplifying your voice, refining your story, and adjusting your message. Your values stay intact, but your story expands to match your evolving mission and the new audiences you're reaching. As you level up, so do the stories you tell. Your mission grows, your goals shift, and your language must reflect that journey.

Take Beyonce's alter ego, Sasha Fierce. She created this persona to embody a more powerful, fearless version of herself on stage. Similarly, as your business evolves and you step onto bigger stages—whether figuratively or literally—your story needs to grow in both presence and clarity. It's no longer just about where you started; it's about where you're going.

Throughout this chapter, we'll explore how evolving your story can unlock fresh opportunities, connect you to new audiences, and reflect the bigger, bolder version of yourself that you're stepping into.

The Importance of Evolving Your Story

As your business shifts, your story should adapt with it. The story that brought you success in the past might not align with where you're heading next—and that's okay. It doesn't mean your old story gets tossed; it might just need a refresh to reflect how you and your business have evolved.

For many of us, changing our story can feel like walking on thin ice. It feels safer to keep doing what's worked, but clinging to an outdated narrative can actually hold you back. If you don't update your story to reflect where you are now, that sense of stagnation creeps in.

Think back to when you first started—remember how uncomfortable it felt to share your story? You'll likely experience that uncertainty again as you step into the next stage of your journey, but it's in that discomfort where real growth happens. And it's not just about the story you tell others—it's about how you see and tell your own story.

Chapter 6: Evolving Your Story as You Grow

Sometimes, we get too focused on certain parts of our story and miss the bigger picture. One morning, I had an epiphany when I found a half-buried arrowhead. It's easy to overlook things when you're only looking for what's obvious.

I find arrowheads because I search for what doesn't fit, while most people focus on what stands out. It's a subtle difference, but that shift in perspective changes everything. When you look for what doesn't fit in your story, you spot the elements that need to change to move forward.

Before you can find the extraordinary, you have to recognize what's ordinary. The same is true for your story—and your audience. When you understand the patterns in your own journey, you can spot where your story is shifting and adapt it to align with what your audience is experiencing. By evolving your story, you continue to connect with them on a deeper level, keeping them engaged as both of you grow.

Overcoming the Challenges of Storytelling Evolution

Evolving your story can be empowering, but it's not always easy. Many business owners face resistance, often rooted in fear—fear of losing what worked, fear of stepping into a new identity, or fear of how the audience might react. Let's

> *Before you can find the extraordinary, you have to find the ordinary and shape your story so it continues to deeply connect.*

break down these common challenges and explore ways to move past them

- **Fear of Losing What Worked**: One of the biggest hurdles is the worry that evolving your story means abandoning the parts that brought you success. It's natural to want to hold on, but clinging too tightly can cause stagnation.

How to Overcome It: Reframe the change as an opportunity. Think of this as building on your past rather than erasing it. Your story isn't about starting over—it's about enhancing what's already there. By evolving your story, you're strengthening your connection with your audience without letting go of what worked before.

- **Feeling Stuck in the "Old You"**: Sometimes, we hesitate to tell a new story because we feel tied to the identity or role we've created—whether that's the scrappy underdog or the solopreneur. But staying stuck in that identity limits your potential.

How to Overcome It: Start small. You don't need to overhaul your story all at once. Begin by making subtle updates that reflect where your business is headed. Gradually weave these into your narrative, and before long, the new version will feel natural and aligned with who you are now.

- **Worrying About Audience Reactions**: A common fear is that changing your story will alienate your audience. The truth is, your audience is evolving, too, and by embracing your next chapter, you're more likely to attract those who align with you while keeping your existing connections.

How to Overcome It: Test the waters. Introduce new elements of your story in smaller doses—through social media posts, blog updates, or one-on-one conversations. See how people react, and fine-tune your story based on their feedback.

- **Embracing the Role of the Hero**: As your story shifts, remember that every hero faces challenges and grows. You're the hero of your own story—and when you embrace that, your audience will be inspired to do the same in their lives.

How to Overcome It: Own your journey. By stepping into the role of the hero, you're not just empowering yourself—you're empowering your audience, showing them what momentum looks like and encouraging them to embrace their own journey.

Upgrading Your Story: From Success to Stadiums

I worked with Carol, who was already crushing it in her business. She was all about leadership for women and had big dreams—she wanted to fill stadiums. But something wasn't clicking.

She had the expertise and the message, but something was missing. Carol hadn't shared the raw, real parts of her story—the moments that shaped her and fueled her mission. Sure, her presentations were polished, but they

Turn Your Story Into Business Gold

lacked that gut-punch emotional connection that turns a speaker from "good" to "unforgettable."

At first, sharing those personal moments felt terrifying. Vulnerability can feel like stepping into the spotlight naked. But here's the thing: being vulnerable doesn't weaken your message—it makes it stronger. It shows people that you're real, giving them something to connect with on a deeper level.

So, we rolled up our sleeves and dug in. We mapped out her values and pinpointed the key moments that proved Carol wasn't just talking about leadership—she was living it. We wove those moments into her story, showing her audience that her mission wasn't just a professional goal; it was a deep-rooted drive to create real change in the world.

The result? Her talks didn't just land—they exploded. Carol became a magnet for the big stages she had always dreamed of. By embracing the full spectrum of her story, she unlocked a new level of connection with her audience and opened doors she never thought possible.

Embracing a growth mindset and continuously moving your story forward is how you set the stage for what's next. As your business expands, so does your audience—and your message needs to expand with it. Your story must evolve to keep up with new trends, shifting expectations, and the people you aim to reach.

Chapter 6: Evolving Your Story as You Grow

Language Shifts for Evolving Your Story

As your story expands, one critical piece is recognizing the power of the words you use—not just in your external narrative, but in how you speak to yourself. Take the common phrase, *"I'm going to be better tomorrow than I am today."* On the surface, it sounds motivating, but it also implies that today isn't enough—that you're not enough right now. This subtle mindset can keep you from fully embracing the story you're living today.

Instead, shift your language. *"I'm amazing today, and I'll be amazing tomorrow too."* This small reframing honors your current strengths while leaving space for continued improvement. Yes, your story is evolving, but that doesn't mean who you are or what you've accomplished today is lacking. By upgrading your words and your story, you're acknowledging your present value as well as your future potential.

This idea ties into the concept of the "solopreneur." Many entrepreneurs proudly adopt this label, but it often reinforces a sense of isolation. It's the story that says you're doing everything alone, even when that's not really the case. Shifting your language from "solopreneur" to something more collaborative, like "building a team" or "leading a business," opens you up to more opportunities and partnerships.

Just like your story, the words you use need to grow with you. Evolving your language isn't just about marketing—it's about how you see yourself and how you position your business. As you refine your story, remember to upgrade both your internal and external language. Words have the power to shape not only how others see your brand but also how you see yourself.

One thing that holds many of us back is getting too hung up on whether every piece of our story is fact in the moment. We hesitate, thinking we have to wait until we've achieved a certain milestone or level of success before sharing that story. But here's the truth: it's your story, and you get to choose how it unfolds.

This isn't about being dishonest—it's about believing in the potential of your story and stepping into the version of it you want to create. Instead of thinking, "Fake it until you make it," try shifting to "telling the truth in advance." It's about claiming the future you want and taking the steps to make it real.

I spoke with a woman recently who was struggling with how to tell her story. I told her, "Choose the ending to your story—it's your story." Whether in business or in life, you have the power to shape the narrative. When you focus on where you're headed, you give yourself permission to act like you're already there.

Think about it like a race car driver: if they focus on the wall, they'll crash. In business, it's the same—focusing on your struggles keeps you spinning your wheels in a cycle of frustration and doubt. But when you shift your focus to success, to the story you want to create, you naturally steer toward that outcome.

Chapter 6: Evolving Your Story as You Grow

Adapting to Shifts in Audience and Market

As your business changes, so does your audience. The story that once resonated with your original niche might not connect as strongly with the new groups you're attracting, and that's completely normal. The key is to anticipate these shifts by staying tuned into your audience's changing needs and interests. Your story should grow alongside them, reflecting your deeper understanding of who they are and what they need. If you don't adapt, you run the risk of losing touch and missing opportunities to engage with them in meaningful ways.

Take Spotify, for example. They started as a music streaming service, but as technology and audience preferences shifted, so did they. Expanding into podcasts and personalized experiences, Spotify stayed true to its core mission: making audio content accessible to everyone. By adapting their story to match the changing needs of their audience, they not only stayed relevant but became a global leader in the audio space.

The lesson here is that staying relevant requires ongoing evolution. Your story needs to grow with the changing landscape of your audience, culture, and industry trends. If you stick to the same story without adjusting, you risk falling behind.

That said, adapting doesn't mean losing your identity. In fact, staying true to your ideals is what makes these shifts feel genuine and aligned. As your audience and the market shift, the key to staying grounded is balancing that change with consistency. That's where your core values come in.

Turn Your Story Into Business Gold

Embrace Change While Staying True to Your Vision

As your business and story adapt, one thing stays solid: your core values. These are the backbone of your brand—the reason people connect with you. No matter how much you adapt, expand, or roll out new offerings, your mission and core beliefs are the foundation that keeps you grounded.

Staying rooted in your purpose keeps your brand authentic, and authenticity builds trust. If you stray too far from what defines you, your story starts to feel hollow, and that disconnect can quickly unravel the relationships you've built.

Balancing change with consistency is key. It's not about throwing out everything that worked—it's about evolving while staying anchored to what matters most. Think of it like a house: your values are the foundation, and your story is the structure. The structure can shift and grow to fit the times, but the foundation stays rock solid. That's what keeps your brand adaptable without losing its core.

Take Patagonia, for example. Over the years, they've expanded their product lines and global reach, but they've never wavered from one core value: environmental sustainability. From recycling programs to raising awareness on environmental issues, they've woven their mission into everything they do. As a result, they've kept their loyal customers while attracting new audiences who align with those same beliefs.

Chapter 6: Evolving Your Story as You Grow

It's also key to know when to update how you communicate your core story. Your standards should stay constant, but how you express them needs to shift as the market, culture, and technology change. It's all about balancing relevance with authenticity—staying true to who you are while adapting to what's happening now.

In today's fast-paced digital world, where consumers are bombarded with brand stories every day, your story has to speak to what your audience cares about today, while still reflecting your essence. Take Apple, for instance. Their story has always been about innovation and creativity, but they've consistently adapted that message to stay in sync with the changing tech landscape. They've never lost sight of their principles, but they've adapted their story to stay fresh and keep their audience engaged.

> *Share the stories that connect with what your audience cares about today.*

As your business grows, your values should be the compass guiding each change. The brands that thrive are the ones that stay connected to their audience, no matter how much they expand.

A socially conscious brand, for example, might expand into new markets, but as long as they keep sustainability or social responsibility at the heart of their story, they'll continue to resonate with customers who share that vision. Growth doesn't come from abandoning your mission—it comes from amplifying it and showing how your purpose evolves with the times.

Using Story Evolution to Expand Opportunities

Updating your story isn't just about staying relevant—it's a powerful way to open doors to new markets, partnerships, and media exposure. It gives your brand the chance to connect with audiences you may not have considered before.

Keeping your story fresh and aligned with where you are today makes you more attractive to new markets, media outlets, and potential collaborators. A dynamic story can unlock opportunities like speaking engagements, media features, and strategic partnerships.

Podcasters and media outlets are always on the lookout for compelling, fresh narratives. By updating your story to reflect your current focus and trajectory, you position yourself as a forward-thinking brand. This also helps align you with partners who share your beliefs, giving you even more opportunities to showcase your expertise to a wider audience.

If your business has shifted focus, launched new products, or entered new markets, evolving your story helps you reposition your brand. This becomes even more important after significant changes in your business—whether you've redefined your mission or moved into a new industry. A well-crafted, updated story ensures your audience understands these shifts and keeps your brand aligned with its new direction.

My own experience with the *Mission Accepted 262 Women's* project is a perfect example of how evolving my story opened new doors. Contributing to this international bestseller gave me the chance to share my story on a global platform, leading to media exposure, partnerships, and speaking engagements I never expected. It even led me to writing this book, which was featured at the Oscars—something I never imagined!

Participating in the project amplified my message and connected me with a broader audience that aligned with my passions, demonstrating how personal growth can open doors to new business opportunities.

Updating your story isn't just a strategy for staying relevant—it's a powerful tool for expanding your reach and positioning your brand to resonate with both current and future audiences.

What's Your Story in 5 Years?

Let's fast forward five years. Your business is booming, your story is polished to perfection, and you're owning the stage (or Zoom) like never before. But here's the question: What does that story look like?

Is it the same story you're telling today, or has it bloomed into something bigger, bolder, and more aligned with where you're headed? Here's the thing: if you're not envisioning your future story, who's writing it? Spoiler alert—it's you.

These are the questions you should be asking at every stage of your business. What does the next chapter of your business look like? Are you aligning with movers and shakers? Are you stepping into that bigger role you've been imagining?

Your story isn't meant to be static—it should grow and evolve, just like you. And if you're not planning for the next level, you're at risk of being left behind. So, step out of your own way and start imagining that bold, fearless version of yourself five years from now.

Because honestly, if you're going to tell a story, you might as well make it epic.

Conclusion

As your business grows, so must your story. Evolving your brand's narrative isn't just about keeping up with changes in your products or services—it's about staying true to your core values while adapting to an ever-shifting world. By updating your story, you stay relevant, attract fresh opportunities, and continue to deepen connections with the people who matter most.

Evolution is about amplifying your mission, refining your story, and holding onto your "why" as you blaze new trails. That's what sets the stage for long-term success.

The most powerful stories? They're the ones lived, breathed, and adapted over time. As you grow, your story follows suit—showing not just where you've been but where you're heading. The businesses that thrive are the ones brave enough to let their story change without ever losing sight of their mission.

Chapter 6: Evolving Your Story as You Grow

So, what's the next chapter in your business and life? Take the time to reflect, refine, and step into that bigger, bolder version of your story. Your audience is ready to connect with the real you—don't be afraid to show them just how far you've come and how much further you're going.

Your story isn't a one-and-done thing—it's a living, breathing reflection of who you are today and who you're becoming. Embrace the journey, take those leaps, and trust that your story will guide you every step of the way.

Key Takeaways

1. **Story Evolution is Essential for Scaling**: As your business expands, your story needs to keep up. An outdated narrative can hold you back and close the door on new opportunities—an evolved story keeps you aligned with your current beliefs, audience, and mission.

2. **Balance Change with Consistency**: Evolving your story doesn't mean abandoning your roots. Staying true to your values while embracing change is the magic formula for authenticity—the key to building lasting trust with your audience.

3. **Evolving Your Story Opens Doors**: A fresh, updated story makes you irresistible to new markets, potential partners, and media opportunities. A forward-thinking narrative helps you reposition your brand and unlock opportunities you didn't even know existed.

4. **Your Story is a Living Entity**: Your story isn't set in stone—it's a living, breathing reflection of who you are and where you're headed. Embrace its evolution as part of your business journey, and let it grow with you.

Mindset Shifts

1. **From Fixed to Dynamic:** Stop thinking of your story as something set in stone. Instead, see it as a living, adaptable part of your business that changes and grows with you. Embracing that shift is key to staying ahead and staying relevant.

2. **From Fear of Change to Embracing New Possibilities:** Worried that updating your story might alienate your audience? Flip that mindset. Adjusting your story is your chance to connect more deeply with your evolving audience and unlock exciting new opportunities.

3. **From Solopreneur to Collaborator:** Let go of the "going it alone" mentality. Your business (and your story) only gets stronger when you lean into collaboration, partnerships, and team-building as you grow.

Action Steps:

1. **Audit Your Current Story:** Take 10 minutes to scan your marketing materials, website, and pitches. Does your message reflect where your business

Chapter 6: Evolving Your Story as You Grow

stands today, or is it stuck in the past? Identify areas that need a refresh to align with your goals and audience.

2. **Identify Key Milestones:** List 3-5 pivotal moments that represent major steps forward in your business—whether it's new offerings, reaching new audiences, or hitting major milestones. Use these moments to update your narrative, making sure they match your brand's direction.

3. **Refine Your Core Message:** Pick one key value that defines your business right now. Rework a part of your story to highlight how this value drives your mission, making sure it's clear in both your internal mindset and external messaging.

4. **Practice Your Refined Story:** In your next conversation—whether with a client, partner, or team—integrate your updated story. Emphasize your recent growth while staying true to your values. Adjust based on their reactions to make sure your story connects.

If you haven't yet gotten your complimentary companion Workbook to go deeper and actually write our your thoughts, shifts, and steps, scan the code to get it now:

Chapter 7
Stories Simplify Sales

Strategic storytelling is powerful and healing. Transform your message, capture hearts and minds, and drive business success with this insightful guide.
– Gayle Nowak, The Story Stylist

We often think of sales as a separate, daunting task—something we either have to "get through" or conquer. But it doesn't have to be a hurdle. Sales is just another step in the larger client journey, one that should flow naturally from the first conversation to closing the deal. Storytelling helps create that seamless thread.

For many, just hearing the word "sales" can trigger memories of awkwardly asking for money as kids, leaving us with an emotional scar that makes selling feel uncomfortable. But here's the thing: we all need money to keep our businesses running, so throwing up our hands isn't an option.

Sales isn't just about closing—it's about understanding whether the person in front of you even needs what you're offering. When you focus on solving problems and sharing stories that resonate, sales stop being scary and start feeling like a natural, engaging conversation.

For a lot of entrepreneurs, selling themselves makes them squirm. When I offered marketing as a standalone service, I saw this all the time—people were fine with marketing, but sales? That was the elephant in the room. Instead of fixing their sales process, they'd constantly tweak their marketing, thinking it would solve the problem. But all it did was create a tangled mess with limited results.

Why Stories Work in Sales

One of the biggest reasons people struggle with sales is that they approach it as if it's all about them. But sales is really about understanding the person in front of you and figuring out how you can help them. Saying, "I'm not a salesperson," doesn't change the fact that sales are essential to keeping your business running—and chances are, you're already better at it than you realize.

Think about it: you naturally talk up movies, books, or your favorite new lipstick without a second thought—recommending the latest business book you've read to a friend who would love it (hint, hint—lol). But when it comes to selling your own services or products, you freeze. You have the skills—it's just a matter of shifting your perspective.

Chapter 7: Stories Simplify Sales

When you focus on how your product or service can improve someone's business, health, or relationships, the conversation flows more naturally. When you believe in the value you're providing, selling feels less like a task and more like a meaningful exchange. By taking the pressure off yourself and focusing on the client's needs, you can detach from the outcome and create space to truly listen to them.

This shift allows you to step back and assess what resonates with your client, helping you adapt your approach to their specific challenges. And that's where storytelling makes all the difference.

When you share a story, you shift the focus from selling to showing. Instead of telling someone what you can do, you're illustrating the real impact your solution has had on others. Stories are a powerful way to showcase the results others have achieved from working with you. They turn sales conversations into genuine exchanges that build trust and connection.

To use storytelling effectively in sales, ask great questions and weave the answers into your narrative. People will naturally share their pains, goals, and frustrations, giving you the material to create a narrative that resonates with their experience and shows them you understand their needs.

> *Effective stories show your audience the results and experiences they will gain with you.*

Listening for Gold in Sales Conversations

Listening is key to crafting a great story in sales. When you tune into your client's pains, goals, and hesitations, you can tailor a story that speaks directly to what they need. Open-ended questions encourage them to talk about their challenges and provide you with the details needed to shape your narrative. Here are a few questions to get things rolling:

- "Can you tell me more about the biggest challenge you're facing right now?"
- "What's keeping you from moving forward with [specific goal]?"
- "What would a successful outcome look like for you?"

As they talk, listen closely for patterns—whether it's time, budget, or uncertainty about the outcome. These are your cues to share a story that speaks directly to their concerns.

For example, if they mention feeling overwhelmed by too many tasks: *"I had a client in the same boat. She felt like she didn't have time for new strategies, but once we broke it down into manageable steps, she found it saved time and helped her focus on what mattered most."*

By sharing stories that reflect the client experience, you build trust and move the conversation forward naturally.

Instead of a hard pitch: *"Joe, you mentioned that not getting more clients was keeping you up at night. I recently worked with Sue, who had the same frustration. She was even considering a career change. We reframed her story and adjusted her marketing strategy, and almost immediately, she signed two new clients. I'm not sure if that would work for you, but what do you think?"*

This approach removes the pressure from the sale and turns it into a conversation, inviting them to collaborate rather than simply being sold something.

Key Listening Tips:

To make sure your stories hit the mark, here are a few key tips to sharpen your listening skills and keep the conversation focused on the client's needs.

- **Mirror back** what the client says. Repeating key points in your own words helps them feel heard and ensures you're on the same page:

    "So, it sounds like your biggest challenge is finding the time to work on growing your business, is that right?"

- **Pause after sharing your story** to give the client space to respond. This lets them process the information and keeps the conversation balanced rather than one-sided.

- **Clarify** if needed. If you're unsure about a specific detail, don't be afraid to ask for more information:

    "I want to make sure I'm fully understanding—can you tell me more about how that's impacting your business?"

By weaving storytelling into your sales process, you're creating a narrative the client can see themselves in, which makes their decision feel smoother and more natural. Let's break down how stories can help at every stage—from handling objections to making the final ask—without adding pressure or stress.

Story-Driven Solutions

Storytelling makes the sales process smoother and more natural in several ways. It helps you build rapport quickly and keeps the conversation focused on the client, not the sale. Instead of pushing your solution, you're guiding them through a narrative that addresses their concerns. Take a connection-first approach.

For example, when objections come up, weaving stories into the conversation can make those objections feel like part of the dialogue, rather than roadblocks. If a client hesitates about budget, you might say, *"I worked with a client who had similar concerns about costs, but after implementing the strategy, she recouped her investment within 45 days."* By sharing this, you're addressing their concern while building trust.

Stories like these shift the focus away from hard selling, allowing decisions to feel more organic and less pressured. The client can see themselves in the story, which simplifies complex choices by offering a clear, relatable path forward. This is how storytelling creates a natural flow, leading to trust and resolution.

Chapter 7: Stories Simplify Sales

Objections aren't roadblocks—they're opportunities to better understand your client and show how you can help. Think of it as a chance to get on the same side of the table, working together to solve their problem. When you listen closely to their concerns, you can offer a story that shows how others with the same challenges found success.

This is where listening becomes your secret weapon. By truly tuning in, you can often anticipate potential objections before they're even voiced. If they're concerned about budget, share a story that addresses that early on. If time is their worry, have a story ready for that too.

For instance, *"I had a client who was worried about the timeline. She needed results quickly and wasn't sure my service would deliver fast enough. But we laid out a plan with clear milestones, and within 30 days, she saw measurable progress—so much so that she wished she had started sooner."* Weaving their concern into a real-life example shows that you understand them. You're not dismissing their objection—you're demonstrating that others have been where they are and still found success.

To keep the conversation collaborative, you might say: *"Based on what you've shared, it sounds like this could address [specific challenge]. What are your thoughts?"* This approach shows that you're not just offering a solution—you're shaping it together based on their needs.

Once you've shared a story-driven solution, the next step is to collaborate with your client to refine it together. This shifts the dynamic from you telling the story to co-creating one with them.

Storytelling not only helps with objections—it softens the "ask." Instead of jumping into a hard sales pitch, introduce your solution through a story: *"I worked with Karla, who had concerns similar to yours. She decided to move forward and saw a 30% increase in client engagement. I'm not sure if that would work for you, but what do you think?"* This keeps the conversation collaborative and reduces the pressure.

Alternatively, you could ask: *"What would you need to feel confident moving forward?"* This makes the close feel like a natural part of the dialogue rather than a high-pressure pitch. You're guiding them through a journey rather than forcing a sale, which makes the decision-making process feel more comfortable and easy.

Weaving stories into the conversation keeps the dialogue open, instead of building up to a single big pitch. It allows you to tackle concerns as they arise and demonstrates that you truly understand their needs.

Transition from Storytelling to the Ask

Storytelling helps you address objections naturally, but moving from handling concerns to asking for a commitment can still feel tricky. To smooth out that transition, keep the conversation flowing by continuing to engage them with questions rather than shifting abruptly to a pitch.

After sharing a story that addresses their concerns, follow up with something like, *"Based on what we've talked about, how do you see this working for your goals?"* This

Chapter 7: Stories Simplify Sales

keeps the dialogue open and invites them to reflect on your solution without feeling pressured.

If they're still unsure, another story can illustrate how someone in a similar position moved forward: *"I had a client who was hesitant because the timing didn't feel right. But she took a small step, and things started falling into place faster than she expected. Within a few months, she hit milestones she hadn't imagined were possible."*

This type of story shows that progress doesn't have to be all-or-nothing, making it easier for them to envision the next steps. You might follow up with a light ask like, *"What do you think would make this decision feel more manageable?"* This demonstrates that you're still focused on finding the best solution for them, not just closing a sale.

Avoid asking confrontational questions like, *"Why wouldn't this work for you?"* These can feel too aggressive, even after building rapport. Instead, keep it collaborative with softer, more positive questions like, *"How can we make this process easier for you?"* or *"What would help make this the right fit?"* These questions keep the conversation focused on working together to solve their problem, making the decision feel less pressured and more like a natural next step.

At the end of the day, it's your call, but asking **how** and **what** rather than **why** keeps the conversation solution-focused and prevents the client from feeling defensive.

Reframing Sales Through Collaborative Storytelling

Storytelling in sales isn't just about getting the deal—it's about shifting from a competitive mindset to a collaborative one. Instead of seeing the sale as something to "win," think of it as working together with your client to find the best solution for their needs.

For example, asking, *"How can we make this work for your timeline or budget?"* shows flexibility and lets the client know their concerns are front and center. You can also use stories to reinforce this collaboration.

Like this: *"A client came to me thinking they had to pick the best provider from a crowded field. Instead, we worked together to create a solution that was perfect for them. It wasn't about competing for their business—it was about finding a path that worked for them."*

Another example comes from Larry, an entrepreneur who completely reframed the sales process with storytelling. Instead of delivering a hard pitch, Larry asked clients about their struggles and then shared stories of how others faced similar challenges and found success.

He might say something like: *"I worked with a client last year who was overwhelmed by managing multiple social media accounts. After trying my strategy, they boosted engagement by 40% and saw a significant increase in sales. Do you think this could work for you?"*

By sharing relatable stories and positioning the sale as a collaborative effort, Larry made it clear he wasn't just selling a solution—he was inviting clients to explore how they could achieve similar success.

Framework for Using Stories in Sales Conversations

Storytelling takes many forms throughout the sales process, but a structured approach can make it more effective. Here's a simple, step-by-step framework for weaving stories into your sales conversations.

Step 1: Build Trust through Relatability

The first step in any sales conversation is building trust, and empathy is one of the fastest ways to do that. Start by sharing a story that shows you understand the client's situation, whether it's personal or from a past client.

For example: *"I worked with a client who was in a similar situation, struggling to connect with their audience. Here's what we did to turn it around."*

Showing that you've tackled similar challenges creates an instant connection. Listening carefully to the person's pain points allows you to share a story that helps bridge the gap between where they are and where they want to be.

Step 2: Present Your Solution through a Story.

Once trust is established, introduce your solution with a story that highlights how it's helped someone hit their goals. Focus on the benefits, not just the features.

For example: *"Tom was juggling multiple roles as an entrepreneur. After using our software, he saved 10 hours a week, freeing him up to grow his business."*

Hearing about someone else's success makes it easier for the client to imagine similar results for themselves.

Step 3: Reframe Objections with a Narrative

Objections are a natural part of the process, and instead of treating them like roadblocks, reframe them with a story.

For example: *"Susan was worried that my process wouldn't fit her timeline. But after our first session, she realized how streamlined it was, and we gathered everything she needed quickly and efficiently."*

Bringing up potential objections through storytelling helps the client feel understood and makes it easier for them to see how your solution addresses their concerns.

Step 4: Share Stories that Highlight Results

To build confidence in your solution, share stories that show real, tangible results.

For example: *"One client was struggling with social media campaigns, but after using my services, she booked two clients within 24 hours."*

This allows the client to picture similar success for themselves without feeling pushed.

Step 5: Transition to the Ask with Confidence

The final step is transitioning smoothly from storytelling to closing the deal. By now, you've built trust, addressed concerns, and shown results, so the ask should feel like a natural next step.

Instead of asking, *"When should we start?"* you might try: *"What would stop us from working together?"* or *"Does it seem like this solution could work for you?"*

These questions get the client thinking about how the solution fits their needs without making them feel like they're being pushed into a decision. It's one thing to talk about the framework, but seeing it in action is where the real understanding happens.

Story-Driven Sales Conversations

Now that you've got the framework down, let's talk about how it plays out in real sales conversations. Storytelling can guide your clients from building a relationship all the way to closing the deal. The key is to keep the conversation going, weaving stories in naturally, and addressing concerns before they even surface.

Indecision is pretty common, especially when clients are facing big decisions that could impact their business. Often, they're stuck because they're afraid of making the wrong choice, even when they know they need help.

Tom knew he needed to make some changes in his business but hesitated to commit. He wasn't sure if

Turn Your Story Into Business Gold

working with me was the right move or if the timing was off.

"I totally understand. I've worked with others in your position. Let me tell you about Anna. She had the same hesitation—unsure if the timing was right. We started small, focusing on her immediate needs. Within a few weeks, the real breakthrough was her confidence. Once she committed, everything started to fall into place. Six months later, she had scaled her business beyond what she thought was possible."

By sharing Anna's story, I helped Tom see that the challenge wasn't just about making a decision—it was about overcoming the fear of making it. Sometimes, just committing to the process is the first big win.

Entrepreneurs, especially those who've been burned before, often worry about whether they'll get their money's worth. So, how do you help them see the value in what you offer?

Amber had worked with coaches before but hadn't seen the results she expected.

"I get it. I've been there myself, spending time and money on solutions that didn't pan out. Recently, I worked with Gina, who had similar concerns. To ease her mind, I offered a satisfaction guarantee—if we didn't make progress in the first month, I'd refund her money. We also set up a weekly goal tracker to measure her progress. By the end of the first month, not only had we hit her goals, but she felt confident enough to commit to six more months. She

Chapter 7: Stories Simplify Sales

realized that the long-term relationship would help her overcome challenges and hit her milestones."

By sharing Gina's story, I addressed Amber's fears about making another poor investment and highlighted the value of building a longer-term relationship.

Sheila had already hit a high level of success but felt stuck. She had a bigger mission in mind but wasn't sure how to take the next steps.

"I totally understand—it's a huge leap into the unknown. I worked with Renee, who had written a book, was speaking regularly, and had launched a course. But she wanted to expand her reach to a bigger audience. Together, we clarified her goals, honed her speaking skills, removed distractions, and shifted her mindset. With a clear strategy, Renee attracted high-value clients and confidently stepped into a bigger role."

By sharing Renee's story, I helped Sheila see that she wasn't alone in feeling stuck, and that with the right strategy and mindset, she could confidently step into her larger mission.

Conclusion

Storytelling takes the pressure out of sales by turning the conversation from a transaction into a relationship. Instead of seeing objections as hurdles, they become opportunities to connect on a deeper level. What could feel like a stressful, high-stakes process turns into a relaxed, flowing dialogue.

By using stories, you make the entire process more natural and collaborative. Stories help you build trust, handle objections, and connect with clients in a way that feels authentic. They shift the focus from just making a sale to solving real problems and delivering real value.

It's also important to remember that a "no" doesn't reflect your personal value. Rejection in sales can feel personal, but it's just part of the process. Instead of seeing it as a failure, step back and reflect on the conversation. What worked? What didn't? What resonated with the client, and what didn't land? This kind of reflection is crucial—it helps you fine-tune your approach for future conversations.

Whether you're using stories to build rapport, present your solution, or smoothly close the deal, storytelling humanizes the sales process. It lets you move away from hard pitches and invites clients into a more collaborative conversation.

As you head into your next sales conversation, remember that the stories you share can do more than just showcase your value—they can make the whole process more enjoyable for both you and your client. Go into it with collaboration in mind, and let your stories guide the way. Every sales conversation is a chance to learn, improve, and refine your approach—no matter how it turns out.

Key Takeaways

1. **Storytelling Shifts Sales from Transactional to Relational:** Stories help make sales feel less like a business transaction and more like a genuine

conversation. You're building trust and keeping things comfortable.

2. **Address Objections with Stories Before They Arise:** Instead of getting tripped up by objections, use stories to handle them before they even come up. It turns potential issues into connection points.

3. **Focus on Value, Not Features**: Skip the technical details—stories let you show the real benefits and outcomes, making it easier for clients to picture their own success.

4. **Every Sales Conversation is a Learning Opportunity**: A "no" doesn't define your value. Each conversation is a chance to learn, adjust, and refine your approach for next time.

Mindset Shifts

1. **From Selling to Storytelling:** Forget about pushing products—focus on connecting through stories. This makes sales less stressful and more of a natural, engaging conversation.

2. **From Objections to Opportunities:** Instead of seeing objections as problems, use them as a chance to build trust and dive deeper into the client's needs with a story.

3. **From Features to Benefits:** Rather than getting bogged down by specs, focus on the real-life

benefits your client will get. It helps them see how your solution fits their life or business.

Action Steps:

1. **Identify Your Core Story:** Reflect on a key personal or professional story that highlights a challenge, solution, and result. Use this as your go-to story in future sales conversations.

2. **Build a Story Bank:** Collect 5-7 client success stories that address common objections like price, time, or value. Organize them for easy reference during sales conversations.

3. **Practice the Soft Ask**: Record yourself pitching a solution and, instead of a direct ask, integrate a story that demonstrates how your solution worked for someone else. Review and refine your approach.

4. **Reframe an Objection with a Story**: Next time a client raises an objection, respond with a story instead of a rebuttal. Reflect on the client's response and adjust your approach for future conversations.

If you haven't yet gotten your complimentary companion Workbook to go deeper and actually write our your thoughts, shifts, and steps, scan the code to get it now:

Chapter 8
When a Story Becomes a Movement

"When women lead with authenticity they create environments where ideas thrive, empowering everyone to achieve their potential."
– Sharon Clark, Transformational Life Coach

Have you ever had one of those conversations that seemed casual, but deep down, you knew it would change everything? That's how it was when I first spoke with Deb Drummond. She was pulling together this ambitious project, bringing 262 female entrepreneurs together to share their stories through summits and a book. Casual enough, right? But then she mentioned Gloria Steinem's name—yes, *the* Gloria, a personal hero of mine—and suddenly, I knew this wasn't just another collaboration. This was going to be something bigger.

I didn't have all the details, but just knowing that Gloria's spirit was in the mix was enough. If she was involved in any way, I was in. Sometimes, that's all it takes—one name, one connection, one spark that makes you a follower before you even realize what you're following.

Here's the thing about movements—they make every story shine a little brighter.

I've heard people spout utter rubbish, like, 'Your story only matters if you're successful.' That nonsense misses the point entirely—we all put our pants on one leg at a time.

What we care about isn't the success—it's the slice of the story that connects us to the person telling it. The part that makes us say, "Yeah, I get that." That's why movements are so powerful; they celebrate those connections, no matter who you are or where you're at. Your story matters because someone out there *needs* to hear it.

The 262 Women's Project has become just that—something massive. It took me with it as it traveled to the Emmys, to Ireland, all over the United States, and physically to the Oscars, of all places. Its scope extended beyond just sharing stories. It's been about creating a movement where each of us is heard, where every story adds to the larger conversation. That's what happens when you link arms with others; you go from being a lone voice to being part of a chorus that's impossible to ignore.

Movements don't silence individual voices—they amplify them. Being part of a movement isn't about giving up your story; it's about watching it grow louder, bolder, and more impactful because of the stories surrounding it. It's about recognizing that while one voice can be powerful, a thousand voices can create real change. Power is in the numbers.

And that's what I want to help you do—take your story, align it with a cause, and build something that resonates far beyond you. Whether you're leading a movement or joining one, the power of your story can change everything. Let's dive into how you can make that happen

From Individual Insight to Collective Action

Have you ever noticed how one spark—whether it's a conversation or an idea—can ignite something huge? That's the power of storytelling. It's not just about sharing your experience; it's about connecting people, bringing them together, and creating something bigger than any one person. Movements start when stories inspire action. And the best part? They don't have to be grand to make an impact.

When a story is told right, it doesn't just sit in someone's head—it pushes them to do something. A good story gets people to stand up, step in, and get involved. It pulls in those who otherwise wouldn't cross paths, all united by a shared goal or vision. That's what movements are built on—stories that connect, motivate, and mobilize.

We all want to feel like we're part of something, right? A powerful story creates that sense of belonging, turning listeners into doers. That's where the magic happens in movements—it's about more than just listening; it's about showing up. When people feel like they're part of a community, they're ready to roll up their sleeves and take action.

The best stories don't just support businesses—they drive causes. Think of it like this: brands that resonate are the ones that turn their mission into a movement. When people can see themselves in your story, they're more than customers—they're advocates. That's how you take a personal story and turn it into something bigger.

So, how do you take your story and elevate it into a movement? It's simple—align it with something people actually care about, something they're willing to get behind. The beauty of this? You don't have to be rich, famous, or flawless. You just need to be real and tap into that connection we all crave. Let's break it down and figure out how your story can spark something bigger.

What Makes a Movement?

At its core, a movement is just a group of people coming together to make something happen. They're fired up about a shared goal, and they're ready to push for real change. Movements come in all shapes and sizes—whether it's fighting for social justice, saving the planet, or changing the way people think about business. What makes them powerful is their ability to rally people and resources to actually *do* something.

Movements are fueled by people who care enough to get involved, building momentum from the ground up. Unlike rigid organizations, movements are flexible. They grow, they adapt, and they thrive because they're driven by

Chapter 8: When a Story Becomes a Movement

passion, not just a business plan. It's not about personal gain—it's about what you believe in and the change you want to see. Now that we've explored what makes a movement powerful, let's dive into how you can take your own story and ignite that kind of collective momentum.

How to Turn Your Story into a Movement

Turning your personal story into a movement isn't about having all the answers. It's about tapping into something real, something that others feel too. Your story matters, but it's the themes and emotions

> *The themes and emotions behind your story are what draw people in to stand with you and get behind you.*

behind it that get people to stand with you. Here's how you take that personal experience and turn it into something that brings others in:

1. Find What People Care About

It starts with looking at your story and finding the moments that connect to bigger, universal experiences—overcoming a challenge, fighting for something you believe in, standing strong when things get tough. These are the moments that make people pause and say, *"I know what that feels like."* That's the connection you're aiming for.

2. Tell It in a Way That Sticks

Your story needs to hit home. Be clear about what happened, but more importantly, make people feel it. The emotional side of your story is what grabs attention and gets people to pass it on. The more authentic, the better—people can tell when it's real, and that's what they'll rally behind.

3. Build a Community Around It

Movements grow because they bring people together. Once you've told your story, invite others to join in. Create spaces—whether it's online or in person—where people can share their own experiences and connect. The more voices, the stronger the movement.

4. Hand Over the Mic

This isn't about one person being in charge. The most powerful movements let other people step up and lead in their own way. Encourage people to add their voices to the mix, and watch the movement grow beyond just your story—it becomes *their* story too.

5. Stay Flexible and Pay Attention

Movements aren't static. They shift, grow, and sometimes head in unexpected directions. You've probably heard people complain that some movements go too far or swing too wide, but the truth is, they often need to. Sometimes the pendulum has to swing far just to move the needle a little.

Think of it like any big change—it feels huge when you're in the middle of it, but looking back, it often seems like just

Chapter 8: When a Story Becomes a Movement

the beginning. That's how real progress works—two steps forward, one step back. But even those small steps make a big difference in the long run.

Movements adapt and grow. The key is staying focused on the bigger picture and being flexible when adjustments are needed. That's how you maintain momentum and keep things moving forward.

Keeping the Momentum: Deb Drummond's Story

Deb Drummond's story is a testament to the power of vision and perseverance. For 30 years, she dreamed of creating a platform where women could be empowered and supported. It wasn't an overnight success—far from it. It took decades of work, persistence, and a deep belief in her mission to bring her vision to life.

For Deb, it wasn't just about building a business; it was about creating a movement. The platform she envisioned was more than a place to share stories—it was designed to uplift and amplify women's voices, to give them the confidence and space they needed to make an impact. Over time, her dream grew bigger, and with every challenge she faced, the vision became clearer.

What makes Deb's journey so powerful is that she didn't let time discourage her. She kept pushing, kept dreaming, and eventually, she saw her vision come together with the 262 Women's project—a platform where female entrepreneurs could unite, share their stories, and inspire each other.

Her story reminds us that movements aren't about immediate results; they're about staying committed, even when the road is long. And once that spark ignites, it can lead to something far bigger than you ever imagined.

When you share your story, you're not just talking about yourself—you're creating a connection that resonates with others. Over time, those connections grow. The more people relate to your story, the more they want to be a part of something bigger. Movements evolve, and while you might start with one simple goal, it can lead to something you didn't even imagine.

Your story can inspire action and when people feel that connection, they want to take ownership of it too. Before you know it, what started as a personal journey turns into something that drives real change, whether in your community or beyond.

Leveraging Storytelling for Impact

When it comes to creating real change, storytelling is your greatest asset. It's not just about spreading information—it's about making people feel something. When you connect with your audience on a human level, you're not just sharing your journey; you're offering them a reason to care.

The key is to make it personal but universal. Whether you're telling a story of overcoming adversity, chasing a passion, or learning from failure, it's the emotion that pulls people in. It's the feeling of *I've been there* that motivates them to take action.

Chapter 8: When a Story Becomes a Movement

Here's the thing—people can spot a fake story a mile away. If you want your story to inspire action, it needs to be real, raw, and authentically yours. It doesn't have to be polished or perfect, but it does need to resonate.

When Deb spent 30 years building her platform, she didn't start with a perfectly laid-out plan. She had a vision, and she kept showing up, sharing her story, and evolving with it. That's how real movements begin—not with perfection, but with persistence.

> *Effective stories are real, raw, and authentically yours.*

Movements take time, and the key to keeping them going is consistency. Whether you're sharing your story with a small group or a massive audience, the message needs to stay clear and consistent. People follow when they know what they're following.

Deb knew this when she started her journey. She wasn't just sharing her story once and hoping for the best—she kept telling it, refining it, and connecting with others who shared her vision. That's what builds trust and loyalty.

As your movement grows, it will change—and that's a good thing. Be open to feedback, adapt when necessary, and let others contribute their stories. A movement is never about one person. The more voices that join in, the stronger it becomes.

Deb's movement wasn't built on her story alone—it thrived because she invited others to take the mic and share their stories. That's how movements evolve and sustain themselves—by creating something meaningful that people are proud to join.

The Follower in a Movement

As movements evolve, they take on lives of their own. And while leaders may spark the initial momentum, it's the followers who keep that momentum going. This isn't just about passive participation—followers in a movement are contributors. They bring their stories, their energy, and their own sense of purpose to the table, shaping the direction of the movement.

When we think of movements, we often picture the people at the forefront—the leaders, the visionaries. The power of any movement isn't just in those who lead, it's in those who follow. Being part of a movement means more than just showing up or being inspired by someone else's story. It's about contributing to a larger cause, finding your own voice within the collective, and adding energy to the momentum.

Having a large following doesn't automatically mean you've built a movement. There's a fine line between gathering an audience and creating something people truly want to be part of. With an audience, people are passive consumers, simply taking in the content. But in a movement, followers are active participants—they bring their stories, their energy, and their purpose, shaping the direction alongside the leader. That's the real difference.

The 262 Women's project has created something beyond a simple group or audience. It's a community where every

Chapter 8: When a Story Becomes a Movement

person matters, and the synergy is what keeps it alive. People don't just watch from the sidelines—they join in, share their stories, and help carry the mission forward. That's the beauty of a true movement—it gives space for everyone to play a part, no matter how big or small.

Being Part of the Collective Energy

There's a special kind of energy that comes from being in a movement where everyone is pushing for the same cause. It's not about individual goals or recognition; it's about contributing to something larger. In a movement, the power of the group amplifies the impact of each individual. That's what separates a movement from a following—the collective effort.

When you're part of something like this, it's not just about following the leader. It's about aligning your personal mission with the movement's goals. You feel seen, heard, and valued for your contribution. The movement doesn't just belong to the leader—it belongs to everyone who steps up and takes part.

Crafting Your Story within a Movement

Telling your story within the context of a movement isn't just about sharing experiences—it's about finding the right way to connect with others and create impact. But how do you do that effectively? Let's break it down into key strategies:

1. The Most Compelling Part of Your Story

Not every part of your story will resonate with everyone, and that's okay. The key is to find the moments that evoke emotion and connection.

- **What moment in your story sparks the most emotion?** Is it a challenge you faced? A realization that changed everything? These emotional turning points are what grab attention.

- **Why should someone care?** This is an essential question. People care when your story speaks to something they've experienced or feared. Focus on universal emotions—fear, hope, resilience—that transcend individual experiences.

For example, if you're part of a movement for gender equality, instead of focusing solely on your personal struggles, connect them to the larger issue by highlighting how your story represents a common experience shared by others in the movement.

2. Balancing Authenticity with the Larger Cause

It's critical to be authentic, but there's a balance between telling your truth and keeping the movement's mission at the forefront. Your story should always align with the larger message you want to send. Here's how to balance that:

- **Keep your core values clear.** Whether your focus is empowerment, resilience, or transformation, make sure that comes through in your story. Authenticity doesn't mean you have to overshare—it means

Chapter 8: When a Story Becomes a Movement

aligning your personal truth with the values that the movement upholds.

- **Weave your story into the movement's purpose.** Use your story as a bridge to the larger cause. How does your experience reflect the collective mission? How can others see themselves in your journey? By doing this, your story becomes not just personal, but part of a collective narrative.

3. Using Different Formats for a Larger Impact

Once you've honed in on the core of your story, it's time to share it—and not just in one place. The more you diversify the ways you tell your story, the more people you'll reach. Here's how to approach different formats:

- **Speaking:** Whether it's on stage, at an event, or in a video, your story takes on a new power when spoken aloud. Focus on delivery—tone, pacing, and body language all play a role in how your message is received.

- **Writing:** Blogs, articles, or even social media posts allow you to dive deeper into your story. The written word lets you layer in details and reflections that might not fit into a speech. Keep it conversational but impactful, with clear calls to action that encourage readers to engage.

- **Social Media:** Platforms like Instagram, LinkedIn, or even TikTok are perfect for quick, digestible versions of your story. You don't have to tell the whole thing—just give people a snapshot that invites them to learn more. Use visuals, captions, and hashtags to amplify your reach and connect with communities that align with your message.

Storytelling in Business and Advocacy Movements

Just like people, businesses and causes know that stories are what build real connections. It's not just about selling products or pushing a cause—it's about tapping into something deeper that gets people to feel and act.

On the business side, look at Ben & Jerry's. Sure, they make great ice cream, but that's not what their loyal community is about. They've taken a stand on big issues like climate change and social justice, weaving those values into everything they do. Their story isn't just about desserts; it's about being a brand that cares about the world. And that's why people stick around—they want to be part of something bigger.

Then there's TOMS. They didn't just sell shoes; they turned every purchase into an opportunity to make a difference. With their "One for One" campaign, they told a story that made people feel like they were doing good just by shopping. Customers weren't just buying shoes—they were buying into the idea that they could help someone else. That story turned into a movement, with people eager to step up and be part of the bigger picture.

On the advocacy side, think about #MeToo. It started with individual voices, but those stories came together to create a global wave of change. It was raw, honest, and impossible to ignore. That's what happens when storytelling taps into something real—it pushes people to act and shifts the conversation on a massive scale.

Whether in business or advocacy, storytelling is the common thread that brings people together and turns ideas into action. While business movements often focus on aligning a product with a purpose, advocacy movements center around collective experiences and social change. Yet, both are fueled by stories that resonate deeply, inspiring others to show up and contribute.

Movements aren't built on products or policies alone—they're built on the stories that make people care enough to do something. Your story has that same potential. When it connects with something bigger, people don't just listen—they show up, contribute, and help push the mission forward.

Conclusion

Movements aren't built overnight, and they don't happen by accident. They start with a story—*your* story—told with purpose, passion, and vision. It's not just about what you've been through; it's about what you believe in and how you inspire others to believe in it. Every movement begins with one person daring to speak up, to step forward, and to share their truth in a way that connects and calls others to action.

Your story is more powerful than you think. When you share it, you're giving others permission to do the same. You're creating space for people to see themselves in your journey, to connect, and to join in the cause. A movement is born when your voice resonates so strongly that it compels others to stand with you—not because they have to, but because they *want* to.

You don't need perfection or a grand plan to start a movement. What you need is the courage to put your story out there, to let it evolve, and to trust that it will bring the right people to you. It's about creating something that others want to be part of, something that lights a fire in them, something that makes them say, *this matters*.

So, if you've ever wondered whether your story is enough, the answer is simple: it is. Every great movement started with one voice, one idea, and one story shared at the right moment. Now, it's your turn. Take what you've lived, what you've learned, and put it out into the world.

Because a movement doesn't wait for permission. It waits for someone bold enough to begin.

Key Takeaways

1. **Stories Build Bridges:** Your story isn't just yours—when you share it, you're building connections that inspire others to act and create something bigger than any one person.

2. **Be Real, or Don't Bother:** People can tell when you're faking it. The more raw and relatable your story, the more deeply it will resonate and motivate others to get involved.

Chapter 8: When a Story Becomes a Movement

3. **Storytelling Is the Heart of Any Movement:** Whether you're in business or advocacy, stories get people to care, act, and stick around for the long haul.

4. **Movements Thrive on Inclusion:** A true movement grows when others feel empowered to share their own stories and shape the direction. Consistency, feedback, and the ability to evolve are what keep it alive.

Mindset Shifts

1. **From Self to Collective:** Stop thinking your story is only about you—it's got the power to kickstart a movement. When it's real, your story can spark action and create lasting change.

2. **Ditch Perfection, Embrace Real:** Forget trying to make your story flawless. The magic happens when you share it raw, relatable, and human—because that's what connects with people.

3. **From Leading to Empowering:** It's not just about your voice. A real movement grows when others are empowered to share theirs. Give others the space to lead and watch your movement evolve.

Action Steps:

1. **Identify Your Story's Core Themes:** Think about the moments in your story that really connect with

others. Whether it's overcoming adversity or finding your purpose, write down three key themes that resonate with a wider audience.

2. **Be Consistent with Your Story:** Pick a platform—whether it's Instagram, LinkedIn, or speaking gigs—and share your story regularly. The more consistent you are, the more trust and understanding you build.

3. **Invite Others to Step In:** Ask people in your community to share their own stories alongside yours. Giving others the chance to speak strengthens the movement and deepens the connection.

4. **Create a Rally Cry:** Craft a short, punchy tagline or message that captures the heart of your story and invites others to join in. Make sure it's something easy to remember that inspires action.

If you haven't yet gotten your complimentary companion Workbook to go deeper and actually write our your thoughts, shifts, and steps, scan the code to get it now:

Chapter 9
Storytelling in the Digital Era

"Embrace change with courage; it's the doorway to growth, new beginnings, and boundless opportunities. Trust yourself, and step forward into your best future."
– Nathalie Chauvel, The AI Success Coach

In today's digital age, storytelling isn't just useful—it's essential. What once was shared over coffee is now broadcast across social media, podcasts, and videos with a single tap. It's fast, it's loud, and sometimes it feels like everyone's shouting into the void—but that's where the fun begins. The right story, told at the right moment, cuts through the noise and sticks.

Stories today aren't just told—they're experienced. With every click, share, and like, they shape perceptions, build communities, and drive sales. They're no longer linear but dynamic and interactive, often shaped by the audience itself through engagement. Even if your audience isn't actively responding, they're absorbing your content and forming lasting impressions.

Before we dive in, let's clear something up: social media isn't all of marketing—it's just one piece of the puzzle. But if you're online, you need a presence, and social media is an excellent place to start. I won't cover every aspect of marketing here; instead, we'll focus on the essentials of digital storytelling. It's about mastering one step at a time, and that strategy works whether you're just starting or already have a plan in place.

Throughout this chapter, we'll talk about platforms—any online space where you can share your story, whether it's Instagram, YouTube, blogs, or so many more. Each one has its own language and style, and learning to tell your story effectively across these spaces is key.

This chapter will show you why digital storytelling is crucial if you want to make an impact. Whether you've been at this for years or are just getting started, knowing how to tell a good story online helps you stand out and build real connections.

Storytelling as Strategy, Not Fluff

One of the biggest misconceptions in business is that storytelling is a "nice-to-have"—something creative to tack onto your marketing plan. But storytelling *is* strategy. Every piece of content you create should have a purpose, and every story you tell should serve an intentional role in your business.

I had a conversation with another business coach who misunderstood this idea. I explained how I help clients use storytelling strategically to attract more business and

Chapter 9: Storytelling in the Digital Era

simplify their marketing. She nodded, but later mentioned she was focused on "strategy," as if storytelling didn't fit into that equation. This is a common mistake—people view storytelling as separate from strategy, but it's integral to it. Your story is the foundation of everything you do.

> *Effective storytelling creates impact and cuts through the noise.*

In today's fragmented digital world, storytelling is how you cut through the noise. It's more than just sharing stories—it's about using them to drive engagement, build trust, and grow your business. People want short, impactful stories that deliver real value. If your story drags, they'll move on.

Technology Innovations: One Step at a Time

Technology has transformed how we share stories. With real-time voice translation and tools making storytelling easier to manage, we're now more connected than ever. But with so many options, it can be mind-boggling. The trick is to start small and add layers as you go, using the right tools to streamline the process.

- **Scheduling Posts**: Plan and schedule your content ahead of time to stay consistent without being online 24/7.

- **Video Editing and Captions**: Simple editing and captions make your content polished and accessible.

- **Transcription**: Convert speech into text easily, whether it's a podcast, interview, or voice memo, giving you multiple content formats.

These are just a few tools to help simplify storytelling. The key is to start small and build up over time.

I recently pushed myself to post one-minute videos across five platforms for 45 days. It wasn't perfect on day one—no captions, no end screens—but each day, I added something new. By day 8, I'd introduced transitions and a smoother posting process. Perfection isn't the goal—momentum is. You'll get faster and better with time, but only if you dive in and start.

AI tools and process automation can help make your routine easier, too. Don't be afraid to ask others for advice or use time-saving hacks. Once your system is in place, you'll manage it with far less effort than you ever thought possible.

Adapting Your Story for Different Platforms

In today's fast-paced world, stories need to be adapted to different channels because each has its own unique style of audience engagement. From Instagram's snappy visuals to YouTube's in-depth narratives, knowing the "language" of each platform is key to digital storytelling success. Before jumping into adaptation, take a moment to reflect on where you stand.

You already have a digital presence, whether you've consciously curated it or not. Take a moment to ask: does

Chapter 9: Storytelling in the Digital Era

your digital footprint truly reflect who you are or who you want to be? This is your opportunity to make sure your story aligns with your values and vision.

Social media can feel like a never-ending reality show, constantly bombarding you with updates and opinions. The trick is learning how to filter through the noise and stay focused. Whether you're loved, hated, or ignored, it's not personal. Recognize this dynamic, find your people, and trust that there's an audience for everyone.

Each online space has its own "language," style, and user expectations. Sometimes a story that resonates on one may not perform as well on another. For example, Instagram thrives on visuals and short, compelling captions where style matters. Your story must be eye-catching in seconds. In contrast, YouTube gives you the flexibility to create anything from quick tutorials to in-depth, visually engaging stories.

Start with one platform that aligns with your audience and plays to your strengths. Master its language, get comfortable with its format, and engage meaningfully with your audience. Once you've built momentum on one, you can expand to another.

Instead of throwing content at multiple platforms and hoping something sticks, take a thoughtful, strategic approach. As you refine your storytelling on one platform, your understanding of your audience will grow, making it easier to adapt your story to others over time.

Choosing the Right Platform

Before you go all-in on digital storytelling, it's time for some real talk: not every platform is your playground, and trying to be everywhere at once will burn you out faster than a viral trend. Start by asking yourself a few key questions to figure out where to begin.

Where's your audience hanging out?

You wouldn't show up at a party if none of your people were there, right? Same goes for digital platforms. Whether it's Instagram, LinkedIn, or something else, find out where your target audience is spending their time, and meet them there.

What content gets you excited?

Love being in front of the camera? Great! Video platforms might be your jam. Prefer typing out killer insights? Then maybe LinkedIn or Twitter is where you'll shine. Stick with what feels fun and natural, because if you hate creating it, your audience will feel that too.

Does your story fit the platform?

Are you all about those bite-sized, snappy posts, or do you prefer deep dives and long-form content? Every platform has its own rhythm, so pick the one that matches your style.

Chapter 9: Storytelling in the Digital Era

What's the end game?

Get clear on your goals. Are you looking to grow a community, build brand loyalty, or flex your expertise? Different platforms serve different objectives, so let your destination guide your choice.

Be honest—how much time and energy can you realistically invest in content creation and engagement? It's better to dominate one platform than to be mediocre on five. Start where you can manage, and grow from there.

The Language of Each Platform

Every digital platform speaks its own language, and to make your story resonate, you've got to know how to "talk the talk." On Instagram, it's all about the visuals—high-quality images or videos paired with short, snappy captions that offer a slice of your story. Twitter, on the other hand, thrives on brevity, so every word has to count.

Then there's LinkedIn. When I first joined, I felt like I was using the wrong fork at a fancy dinner. It's still conversational, but with a professional slant. Stories here need to be structured, thoughtful, and geared toward building credibility and networking.

The key is to understand the vibe of each platform and adjust your tone, style, and story length while staying true to your core message. As you adapt, consistency is the secret sauce. Keep your message aligned, and your audience will recognize you no matter where they find you.

Consistency is Everything

Whether your audience finds you on Instagram, Twitter, YouTube, or your website, your message needs to be cohesive and recognizable. Consistency builds trust, and trust is the foundation of strong, lasting relationships.

Think of social media like TV ads—it's not always about making an instant sale. It's about staying on people's radar, reminding them who you are and what you do. When the time comes for them to need your product or service, you'll be their first choice because your consistent presence has kept you top of mind.

But consistency doesn't mean posting 24/7. It's about finding a rhythm that works for you and your audience. Set a schedule that fits your life, not the other way around. For example, I set aside one day a month to plan and schedule content. That way, I'm not scrambling every day to figure out what to post. I can still add fresh content as I'm inspired throughout the week without the daily pressure.

Tips to Stay Consistent Without Burning Out:

1. **Batch Your Content:** Block off one day a month to create a month's worth of content. This way, you can focus on videos or other fresh content during the week without stressing about coming up with something new every day.

2. **Leverage Content Schedulers:** Schedulers and calendars can help you automate posts. Use them to free up your time instead of scrambling for daily content.

Chapter 9: Storytelling in the Digital Era

3. **Avoid Robotic:** Always focus on providing value. People are watching—are you posting memes that fill space, or are you sharing real gems and insights that speak to people's pain points and dreams? Your audience can tell when your content sounds forced. Make sure every post connects to something deeper, whether it's a personal lesson or insight that links to your brand's message.

4. **Start with Manageable:** Commit to posting three days a week, like Monday, Wednesday, and Friday. Once you've got that down, add more days if it feels right. Or, focus on one platform daily, and keep others at three days a week. You don't need to do everything at once—start small, then scale as you grow comfortable.

Consistency isn't about gaming the algorithm—it's about showing up regularly and making sure your message resonates with those who do see it. Most of your audience won't see every post, so feel free to post multiple times a day if you have the bandwidth. The key is finding what works for you and staying flexible as you adjust over time.

Leveraging Repetition Without Losing Creativity

There are so many facets to what you do and what you know. It's not about struggling to find content—it's about narrowing it down. I talk about storytelling all the time, but that's the umbrella: I can apply it to branding, sales, marketing—everything ties back to using stories as the foundation for your business.

The key is showing your audience different sides of the same coin. I tell stories about storytelling—how it builds emotional connections, strengthens a brand, and boosts sales. Every angle reinforces the same message but offers something new. That's the beauty of repetition—it's not about saying the same thing over and over, but finding fresh ways to keep your core message alive.

It reminds me of a networking event I attended. The founder proudly proclaimed, "We do things differently—none of that stuffy introduction. We have real conversations." Sounds promising, right? But as soon as the event kicked off, it was the same old routine. Worse, it felt like the regulars were just marking their territory, trying to show the new faces that they were in charge. No matter how "different" it was supposed to be, it fell flat because it was just more of the same.

That's what happens when you're not intentional with your messaging. If you keep throwing out the same line without creativity or purpose, people stop paying attention. But if you're deliberate, you can tell your story in countless ways, keeping your audience engaged. Each time you present it, they see a new facet. The trick is staying true to your core message while keeping it fresh.

Building Engagement Through Digital Storytelling

Engagement is the lifeblood of digital storytelling. The beauty of digital platforms is that they allow for real-time, two-way conversations between you and your audience.

Chapter 9: Storytelling in the Digital Era

This interaction is what sets digital storytelling apart from traditional, static media.

Through likes, shares, comments, and live interactions, you can connect with your audience on a deeper level. When people feel like they're part of your story, they're more invested—and that connection turns into brand loyalty.

The key to building engagement is to stop thinking of it as broadcasting a message. Instead, open the door for conversation and invite your audience to join the narrative. Digital platforms make storytelling more interactive than ever. Whether it's through Instagram polls, Twitter threads, or live Q&A sessions, these tools let you bring your audience into the action.

Even if someone isn't commenting or liking, it doesn't mean they're not engaging. Many people absorb your content quietly, thinking about it long after they've scrolled past. Your job is to keep the door open—engagement builds over time, and consistency is key.

Ask for opinions, get feedback on a project, or crowdsource something as simple as choosing a color for your next design. These questions don't have to be complicated, but they show that you value your audience's input. Persistence is part of the game, so keep asking—even if responses don't pour in immediately.

To really engage your audience, give them a role in your story. Ask them to share their experiences or create content around your product or service. When people feel like they're part of the action, they move from just watching to actively participating.

> *Invite your audience into the story and conversation as you build consistently over time.*

Contests, challenges, and hashtag campaigns are great ways to invite participation. Not only does this engage your current followers, but it also expands your reach as they share within their own networks.

Think of engagement like a "design-your-best-cupcake" contest or gathering time management tips—whether visual, written, or a mix of both, these relatable activities pull people into your story without feeling like a corporate campaign.

If you want to truly connect with your audience, start by picking one type of content and stick with it for a while. Maybe it's videos—commit to doing them for 45 days straight. At first, it may feel clunky, but over time, you'll get faster, shake off the fear, and improve. Focus on mastering one activity, then branch out once you've nailed it. This builds confidence, helps refine your skills, and makes storytelling feel more manageable.

Once your audience is involved, the next step is keeping your digital storytelling authentic and impactful. In the final section, we'll cover best practices for creating compelling, visually-driven stories that resonate across platforms.

Best Practices for Digital Storytelling

With so many opportunities on digital platforms, it's easy to feel perplexed. But there are simple steps that will help

Chapter 9: Storytelling in the Digital Era

your stories stick. In a world full of noise, your storytelling needs to be concise, visually strong, and, most importantly, real.

Audiences are bombarded with content daily, and they can spot inauthenticity from a mile away. Stick to your voice, your mission, and your values. You don't need to overshare personal details, but your audience should feel like they're connecting with the real you.

Being real means embracing imperfections. People are drawn to behind-the-scenes, unfiltered moments—especially on platforms like Instagram and TikTok. Challenges are often more relatable than successes, and sharing those moments humanizes your brand.

Visuals are where digital platforms shine. High-quality images, videos, and infographics grab attention and make your message more shareable. Whether it's an Instagram reel, a well-produced YouTube video, or an eye-catching infographic, each piece of content should have a clear role in your narrative. Show behind-the-scenes moments or create educational content—just make sure each visual adds meaning to your story.

Keep it short and sweet. You've got seconds to make an impact, so trim your story to its essentials. Whether it's a tweet, a caption, or a short video, pack as much value or emotion into that limited space as possible.

Practice refining short-form content by writing a 140-character story or creating a 15-second video that distills your brand's message. The more you practice, the better you'll get at making every second count.

Conclusion

Digital storytelling isn't about ticking boxes or throwing content at the wall—it's about creating an experience that makes your audience stop mid-scroll and pay attention. You need to do more than just tell your story; you need to captivate, engage, and bring your audience into the action.

Think of your audience as co-stars, not spectators. They're liking, sharing, commenting, or maybe quietly observing. When you let them see the real, unscripted, messy side of your business or brand, you create a connection. So go ahead—flirt with the camera, be silly, get raw.

Consistency doesn't mean being a broken record; it means staying true to your message while finding new ways to express it. Keep them guessing! Whether it's cheeky Instagram captions or heartfelt YouTube stories, keep your audience engaged without losing who you are.

And don't underestimate the power of visuals. A behind-the-scenes clip, a quick reel, or even a snapshot of your workspace? That's the real gold. Visuals are the gateway to your story. They appeal to every kind of learner: visual, auditory, and even infographic lovers. Mix it up and give them something to feast on.

The bottom line? Storytelling is about connection. It's about showing up authentically and saying, "This is me. Let's do this together." Sure, some days it might feel like you're talking into the void—but keep going. Engagement doesn't always happen overnight, but showing up as your true self will pay off.

Chapter 9: Storytelling in the Digital Era

Digital storytelling is your chance to build a narrative that evolves with you and your audience. With the right blend of strategy, playfulness, and authenticity, your stories will make waves—and your audience? They'll be right there beside you.

Key Takeaways

1. **Digital Storytelling Is About Connection**: It's no longer a one-way street. Involve your audience in the conversation to create meaningful, long-lasting connections.

2. **Visuals Are Crucial**: Visual storytelling helps you cater to multiple learning styles and keeps your audience engaged in a world with short attention spans.

3. **Consistency Across Platforms**: Your story should be recognizable no matter where it's told. Maintaining a coherent brand voice and narrative is key to building trust with your audience.

4. **Adaptation Is Essential**: Tailor your story to the platform you're using, but always stay true to your brand's core message. Not all platforms are the same—adapting without losing your essence is key to success.

Mindset Shifts for Digital Storytelling

1. **From Long-Form to Short-Form**: Stop thinking stories need to be long to be impactful. Bite-sized stories that deliver value quickly can be just as powerful in today's digital world.

2. **From Passive to Interactive**: Digital storytelling is no longer passive. Think of it as a conversation. Your audience wants to engage and feel part of the story, so invite them in.

3. **From Fear of Technology to Embracing It**: Let go of any reluctance to embrace digital storytelling tools. Platforms like Instagram, YouTube, and podcasts offer endless possibilities to bring your story to life in ways that can reach a wider audience.

Action Steps for Digital Storytelling

1. **Audit Your Brand's Story**: Reflect on whether your current storytelling aligns with your brand's core values and mission. Are you sharing authentic, compelling stories that resonate with your audience?

2. **Pick One Platform for 45 Days**: Focus on mastering one platform or content type, like video. Use this period to work out the kinks, get comfortable, and improve your storytelling skills.

3. **Use Visuals Intentionally**: Start incorporating more high-quality visuals into your content. Whether it's

Chapter 9: Storytelling in the Digital Era

behind-the-scenes clips, infographics, or reels, ensure each piece serves a purpose in telling your brand's story.

4. **Invite Your Audience to Participate**: Get your audience involved by asking for feedback, running challenges, or encouraging user-generated content. Make them feel like they're part of the story and create opportunities for meaningful engagement.

If you haven't yet gotten your complimentary companion Workbook to go deeper and actually write our your thoughts, shifts, and steps, scan the code to get it now:

Chapter 10
Mindset in Action

"Your mindset influences your story, and your story determines your future, so make sure you write yourself in as the hero of your own story."
- Margaret (Peggy) Cameron,
Cameron Leadership Development

If your business isn't fun, something's not right. Just like a great relationship, it won't be perfect every day, but you should still end the day with a smile, knowing it's worth it. Too many entrepreneurs hit burnout, lose hope, or drain their bank accounts because they're doing all the wrong things. It's easy to feel like you're in a jungle, hacking through vines but not moving forward.

That's where mindset comes in. We've all heard the "3 feet from gold" story—the one where you're told to keep digging because success is just around the corner. I've always disliked that story. It's mostly used by people selling expensive programs that don't work, trying to convince you that the problem is you, not their flawed system.

Turn Your Story Into Business Gold

Here's the thing: Most people are spinning their wheels in the wrong 80%, focusing on things like tweaking their website, adjusting branding colors, or chasing perfection. Meanwhile, the real movers and shakers? They're laser-focused on the 20% that actually drives results: knowing their audience, mastering their messaging, and dialing in sales strategies that work. This is where mindset and strategy become inseparable.

The **80/20 rule**, known as the **Pareto Principle**[3], means that most of your results come from a small portion of your efforts. The businesses that succeed focus on what matters most: using their energy wisely. But the 80% that fail? They're spreading themselves too thin. The 80/20 rule is more than just a productivity hack—it's a mindset shift that guides you to double down on what actually grows your business.

So, how do you stay in the top 20%? It all starts with mindset. And not just any mindset—one that's sharp, flexible, and resilient enough to handle setbacks and unexpected challenges. This chapter isn't about a magic formula for success; it's about getting your mind right and being able to coach yourself through challenges, setbacks, and doubts.

> *Mindset shapes everything and fuels your success.*

Mindset shapes everything—the way you talk to yourself, the stories you choose to believe, and how you handle setbacks. Do you see failure, or do you see a stepping stone? Every time you shift your mindset, you're rewriting

---

[3] Pareto, Vilfredo. Cours d'économie politique. F. Rouge, 1896.

Chapter 10: Mindset in Action

your story. This chapter is about helping you craft the story you want to live, starting with a mindset that fuels your success.

Recognizing the Story You're Telling

Before you can rewrite your story, you've got to recognize the one you're telling yourself. Like it or not, we all carry around narratives that shape how we show up in life and business. Some stories push us forward, but a lot of them hold us back.

Let's focus on those limiting stories—the ones where you're the underdog who never wins or the "I'm just not cut out for this" character. These stories dig their claws in, especially when tied to past failures or tough experiences. But here's the thing: they're just that—stories. And the beauty of stories is that they can be rewritten.

For years, I was stuck in the trauma of trying out for the boys' 8th-grade basketball team. It wasn't just about the boys shoving me around—it was the story I had internalized. I was the girl who stood up for something and got crushed by the system. For the longest time, that narrative drained me. I couldn't move past it. But one day, I realized that it wasn't the whole story—it was just one chapter. Once I saw that, everything shifted.

The first step in shifting your mindset is calling out the stories that are holding you back. What's the narrative running through your head? Maybe it's "I'm bad at sales" or "I'm not cut out to lead." You can't rewrite a story until you acknowledge it.

So, what's the story you're living right now? Are you in charge, or are fear and self-doubt still writing the script? There's no shame here—it's not about beating yourself up for the story you've been telling. It's about seeing it, so you can change it.

Rewriting the Narrative

Once you've identified the story that's been holding you back, it's time to rewrite it. The beauty of being human is that we get to decide how we interpret our experiences—how we frame the events that shape us. Just because something went wrong doesn't mean the story's over. In fact, that's often where the good stuff begins.

The first step in rewriting your narrative is to look at the situation with fresh eyes. Instead of seeing your setbacks as failures, start viewing them as lessons. Every challenge you've faced has taught you something—even if it's just what *not* to do next time. That's powerful, because now you can build a new story based on growth, not defeat.

For years, I saw my basketball experience as a loss—a failed attempt to stand up for myself and other women. I focused on the frustration of being unheard and discounted. Eventually, I realized the real story was that I had the courage to show up and take a stand for what I believed in. That's the story that has power, and it's the one I choose to carry with me into the future.

Rewriting your narrative doesn't mean ignoring the hard parts or pretending everything was great. It means shifting the focus to what you learned, how you grew, and how

Chapter 10: Mindset in Action

those experiences can fuel your next move. It's about stepping into a new role—one where you're the hero of your own journey.

What's the story you want to tell moving forward? How do you want to show up in your business? Maybe the narrative isn't "I'm bad at sales" anymore. Maybe it's "I'm a work-in-progress, learning and improving with every pitch." Rather than "I'm not cut out to lead," how about "I'm figuring out what kind of leader I want to be."

This is your story, and every day is a new opportunity to edit and revise it. You get to choose how it unfolds. So, rewrite the narrative, and make sure it's one that pushes you forward instead of holding you back.

Navigating the Unknown

Now that you've started rewriting your story, you'll find that progress is seldom linear, and success rarely comes without bumps in the road. The important thing is learning to trust the process, even when it feels uncomfortable or uncertain.

No one is immune to self-doubt, fear, or setbacks—they're part of the journey, whether you're running a business, growing as a leader, or simply navigating life. The difference between those who push through and those who get stuck isn't having all the answers. It's trusting that they'll figure things out along the way.

If those who push through don't have the answers, they know where to seek help. A fellow entrepreneur said to me,

"You seem like a woman of substance." I laughed and paused, then replied, *"I don't know about that, but I do know that I have a long line of women of substance behind and beside me."* That is a powerful combination.

When I was stuck in my old narrative, I knew my beliefs were limiting me. But it was hard to see the forest for the trees, and it took time to unravel my own twisted branches. Sometimes, you have to keep moving forward without knowing exactly what the next step looks like. That's where trusting the process comes in.

So, how do you stay grounded when things feel shaky? Anchor yourself in the story you're creating. Remind yourself why you started and where you're headed. Lean into the messy middle because that's where the real growth happens. When you trust the process, you give yourself permission to take imperfect action, to learn as you go, and to rewrite your story as needed.

Trusting the process isn't about blind faith—it's about trusting yourself. You have the resilience, creativity, and grit to handle whatever comes next. So, don't rush the process, and don't abandon your story just because the next chapter isn't perfectly clear yet. Trust that you're on the right path, and keep moving forward.

Keep Sane and Find Your Community

Finding a community is like grabbing a life raft in the middle of the ocean—there are countless benefits to finding your tribe. But searching for the right community can feel like hunting for a needle in a haystack. You'll dip

Chapter 10: Mindset in Action

your toe into a few groups and quickly realize what works and what doesn't. Each time you join a new community, you get clearer on who you are, what you stand for, and what you won't tolerate. It's like a gymnasium for your "refinement" muscle.

Eventually, you'll hit the jackpot and find people who not only support your growth, but challenge you to stretch beyond what you thought was possible. And when that happens, be grateful and buckle in for the entrepreneurial delight.

Sometimes, finding the right people means walking away from others. If someone is putting you or others down, it's time to sideline that group. If the environment feels awkward or out of sync, it rarely improves—best to move on. When a group's energy or values clash with yours, sticking around will slowly chip away at your self-esteem and wear you down.

Every community has its own personality. The good news is there are endless options out there. The bad news? There are endless options out there. You might love a community that fits where you are now, only to find you've outgrown it while they've stayed the same. Chalk it up to a learning experience and start again to find your people.

The right community will lift you up, challenge you, and help keep you aligned with the person you're becoming.

Get to Your Roots

Finding community is only one piece of the puzzle. To fully rewrite your story, you've got to get to your roots. This is where the deep work happens—digging into your past to understand what's been driving you, and why.

Think of it like untangling knots. The beliefs and behaviors that shaped you didn't form overnight. They've been building over time, influenced by your upbringing, experiences, and the stories you've told yourself along the way. To move forward, sometimes you have to go back and explore those old roots.

Ask yourself: What are the recurring themes in your life? Do you notice certain patterns—like self-sabotage, avoiding confrontation, or constantly doubting yourself? These patterns didn't just show up out of nowhere; they're tied to something deeper. And when you can identify what's at the root, you can start pulling those weeds out.

This isn't about dwelling on the past or blaming yourself for how things have been. It's about understanding how those roots shaped your behavior and how they've impacted your business and life. Once you're aware of those patterns, you can make the conscious decision to change them.

When you dig into your roots, you might not like everything you find. But that's the point. Growth doesn't happen without discomfort. The silver lining? Once you've unearthed what's been holding you back, you're free to plant something new in its place. The clearer you are about your foundation, the stronger you'll grow.

Chapter 10: Mindset in Action

Look for Patterns in Your Stories and Behavior

Now that you've done some digging, it's time to look for patterns in the stories you've been telling yourself—and the behaviors that follow. Whether you realize it or not, recurring themes shape the way you respond to challenges, opportunities, and setbacks.

Start by asking yourself: What keeps coming up? Maybe it's the story that you're not good enough or that you have to work twice as hard as everyone else to see results. Perhaps you're constantly waiting for the other shoe to drop, expecting that good things won't last. Whatever the narrative, chances are it's played out more than once.

These patterns don't just show up in your thoughts—they show up in your actions, or inactions. Maybe you tend to hold back from taking risks, even when opportunities are right in front of you. Or perhaps you overcompensate, throwing yourself into work to prove your worth, only to end up burned out. These behaviors are directly tied to the deeper stories you're carrying.

The good news? Once you've identified the pattern, you can change it. The key is to consciously recognize the behavior, acknowledge where it came from, and choose how you want to respond next time. It's not about flipping a switch overnight—it's about gradually creating new, healthier patterns that support the person you're becoming.

Each time you interrupt an old story, you open up space for a new one. Over time, these small shifts will compound, changing not just your behavior but your entire approach to life and business.

Dream and Create Bigger

Now it's time to stretch your vision—dream bigger than you've ever allowed yourself. Most people limit themselves, not because they lack ability, but because they can't see beyond their current circumstances. They dream small, set safe goals, and aim only for what feels possible in the moment. But if your dream doesn't scare you—even just a little—it's probably not big enough.

> *"Stretch your vision and dream bigger than you've ever allowed yourself."*

So, what would your business, your life, and your impact look like if you allowed yourself to dream beyond realistic'? Magic happens—not in playing it safe, but in letting yourself envision a future that feels out of reach. The irony is, once you start thinking bigger, your actions and opportunities will start aligning with that expanded vision.

When you push yourself to dream beyond limitations, you'll start finding solutions and paths you didn't see before. Opportunities will begin to appear, and people who can help will show up on your doorstep.

Creating a bold, visionary story for your future can feel daunting, especially when it's all still taking shape in your mind. How do you start? Start by imagining your life and business five years from now. Picture the impact you want to make, the clients you want to serve, and the life you

Chapter 10: Mindset in Action

want to live. Don't worry about the "how" just yet; this vision is meant to stretch your thinking and open up possibilities.

Now, break that five-year vision down into smaller pieces. Start with one year: What major milestone or project could you accomplish in the next year that brings you closer to that vision? It doesn't have to be perfect, but it should be bold enough to push your limits and challenge you to grow.

From there, narrow your focus further: What can you achieve in the next three months? These should be practical steps that give you real experience and wins under your belt. Finally, zoom in to the one-month mark: What specific actions can you take over the next 30 days to make progress? Whether it's launching a new product or dedicating time to learning a new skill, the idea is to take consistent, intentional steps—small wins that bring you closer to your bigger story.

The beauty of this process is that it teaches you to dream big while also mastering the small, actionable steps that build toward that vision. As you move through each step, you'll gain the confidence and clarity to refine and expand your story even further.

Telling Your Story as a Journey

Now that you've laid out your bigger vision and broken it down into steps, it's time to start telling that story—not just to others, but to yourself. The key to making your story compelling is to frame it as a journey with steps that show growth, challenges, and progress toward a clear goal.

Think of your story as unfolding in chapters—each one building on the last. You're not waking up one day and achieving everything overnight. You're moving through highs, lows, lessons, and pivots. It's not just about where you're headed; it's about the transformation that happens along the way. The messy middle is where self-doubt creeps in and your resilience gets tested, but it's also where you prove your strength and push through.

The beauty of storytelling is that you get to decide how your story goes—from beginning to end. You're the main character here, and how you frame your experiences shapes how you see yourself and what's possible. We all deal with doubts and fears, but like a race car driver, it's about focusing on the next curve and the finish line, instead of getting stuck in the wreckage behind you.

While the big vision is important, don't forget to celebrate the wins along the way. Every small milestone adds momentum to your story. These moments show that you're not just waiting for some big breakthrough—you're already living the journey, and each step is bringing you closer to the end goal.

Through it all, keep linking each chapter of your journey back to the bigger picture. Every win, every setback, every challenge is part of the larger narrative you're creating for your life and business. Even when things get tough, remind yourself how each piece fits into your overall growth, success, and impact.

Creating a Future-Oriented Narrative

Self-coaching through storytelling helps you reflect on the past while envisioning the future you want to create. Each time you revisit your story, you gain clarity on both where you've been and where you're headed. By reframing limiting beliefs and pushing through them, you're actively designing your next chapter.

Ask yourself: Where do I want to go? What story do I want to be telling five years from now? How can today's experiences shape that future? This forward-thinking mindset shifts you from reacting to life's challenges to proactively creating opportunities. Every decision and action becomes part of the new story you're writing for yourself.

Instead of waiting for external circumstances to change, self-coaching puts you in control. If you catch yourself telling an old, limiting story—like *"I can't do this"* or *"I always mess up"*—you have the power to flip the script. You're in the driver's seat, reshaping setbacks into opportunities for growth.

Like any skill, self-coaching is a muscle you build over time. The more you practice rewriting your narrative, the stronger that muscle becomes. You'll start to catch negative patterns faster and redirect your energy toward a bigger, more empowering story.

Practical Techniques to Embed Your Vision

To make self-coaching part of your routine, try incorporating these practices:

- **Journaling**: Write out your vision for the future. What does the next chapter of your story look like? Go deeper—what kind of leader do you want to be? What values do you want to live by?

- **Vision Boards**: Keep your bigger story front and center with a visual representation of your goals. Seeing those images daily is a powerful reminder of where you're headed.

- **Visualization**: Mentally rehearse your success. Picture yourself achieving your goals, and feel the excitement of stepping into that next chapter. By visualizing it, you embed the vision into your mind, reinforcing your new story.

By embedding these practices into your routine, you're actively shaping your life. Every time you write, visualize, or reflect, you're reinforcing that you're the hero of your journey, steering your story toward the future you want to live.

Conclusion: Taking Mindset into Action

By now, you've seen how powerful your mindset can be in shaping not only the story you tell yourself but also the one you share with the world. This chapter has been about more than just recognizing old patterns or reframing setbacks—it's been about taking deliberate, intentional action to change the way you think, behave, and grow.

Each time you rewrite an old narrative, challenge a limiting belief, or choose to dream bigger, you're reclaiming your power and stepping into the driver's seat of your own journey. You're no longer just reacting to the circumstances around you—you're actively shaping the road ahead. And that's where real transformation begins.

Whether it's through storytelling to understand your past, journaling to cement your vision, or visualizing your next bold move, remember this: mindset is not a one-time shift. It's an ongoing practice—a daily commitment to becoming the person you want to be and creating the future you want to live. Every small step forward strengthens the foundation of the bigger story you're building.

Your mindset is your most powerful tool, capable of transforming every chapter of your life. Use it to reflect on the past and boldly shape what comes next. The next chapter is yours to write. And the future? It's ready for the story only you can tell.

Key Takeaways:

1. **You Control Your Story:** Mindset isn't passive—it's a tool you can actively use to shape your narrative. You have the power to reframe past experiences and create a future vision that aligns with your true potential. Every day, you decide what story you're telling and what direction you're headed.

2. **Trust the Process, Even When It's Messy:** Progress is rarely linear, but staying connected to your long-term vision will keep you moving forward. Trust yourself, and embrace setbacks as part of the journey, knowing each challenge contributes to growth and resilience.

3. **Find and Lean on Your Community:** Surround yourself with people who lift you up and challenge you to be better. The right community will help you stay grounded and support you when self-doubt or fear creeps in.

4. **Mindset is a Practice, Not a One-Time Fix:** Building a powerful mindset takes ongoing effort. Whether it's through journaling, visualization, or self-coaching, embedding these practices into your daily routine helps you stay aligned with your bigger story and empowers you to make bold moves toward your goals.

Mindset Shifts:

1. **From Limiting Beliefs to Empowering Narratives:** Recognize limiting stories you've been telling yourself—like "I'm not good enough" or "I can't do this"—and rewrite them. This allows you to see setbacks as opportunities for growth instead of roadblocks.

2. **From Waiting to Trusting:** Many people wait for everything to make sense, but the real shift happens when you learn to trust the process, even when the

path ahead isn't clear. This shift allows you to move forward with confidence.

3. **From Perfectionism to Progress:** Waiting for the "perfect" time keeps people stuck. Focus on taking small, intentional steps. Progress is the goal.

Action Steps

1. **Journal Your Current Story**: Write down the story about your business, challenges, or personal growth. Include both the wins and the struggles. Once it's on paper, look for areas where you can reframe the narrative to be more empowering. This practice will help you see patterns and reveal limiting beliefs.

2. **Create a Vision Board**: Map out your long-term goals visually. Include images, words, and symbols that represent where you want to go in your business and life. Place it where you see it daily to keep your bigger vision top of mind.

3. **Reframe a Recent Setback**: Think about a recent challenge and reframe it. What did you learn from the experience? How can it push you toward growth? Write down how this moment is a stepping stone rather than a failure, and reflect on the new opportunities it opened up for you.

4. **Set 3-Month Goals**: Break your bigger vision into smaller, manageable steps. Set clear goals for the next three months that align with the long-term

Turn Your Story Into Business Gold

story you're creating. Make sure these goals challenge you but also feel achievable—small wins will help you build momentum and stay on track.

If you haven't yet gotten your complimentary companion Workbook to go deeper and actually write our your thoughts, shifts, and steps, scan the code to get it now:

Chapter 11
Craft the Story That Only You Can Tell

"Your story has immense power, what you do with it can move mountains and change lives".
– Bri Campano, The Podcasters Life Jacket

At some point, each of us faces the same choice: let the world write our story or take control of the pen. Most people are content to let others shape how their story unfolds—but not you. You're here because you know it's time to take charge of your own narrative.

Your story is the blueprint of who you are and the roadmap to who you're becoming. It's the key to connecting with others, growing your business, and—most importantly—proving to yourself that you're capable of far more than you think.

When I committed to writing this book in 45 days, I had no perfect plan. I had doubts, but I also had a vision. That's where your journey begins—with the decision to tell your story, even if you don't have every step laid out. The important part isn't knowing exactly how it will unfold but making the commitment to start.

Writing a book is a lot like building a business or crafting a personal narrative. There's no straight path, and every decision is a part of the unfolding story. What matters most is showing up consistently and trusting that each action, no matter how small, moves you forward.

Your storytelling journey is about more than just owning your past—it's about intentionally crafting the future you want to live. And to do that, there are specific steps that help you build momentum and create the story you want to tell. Whether you're building your brand, growing personally, or leading a business, the process is the same: defining your vision, taking focused action, sharpening your edge, curating your environment, and mastering your emotions.

These steps are more than concepts—they're tools you catn use to shape your journey. Now, let's dive into how they guided me through writing this book, how they help my clients, and how they can guide you in crafting the story only you can write.

Step 1: Define Your Destiny

Before I started writing this book, I needed to get clear on what it was really about. It wasn't just about storytelling; it was about empowering people—especially women—to take control of their narrative. My vision was to give readers the tools to own their story and use it strategically to build

Chapter 11: Craft the Story That Only You Can Tell

something real. Without that clarity, the project would have felt aimless.

Whatever you're building—whether it's a business, brand, or movement—you need to understand the reason behind it. Your vision gives you purpose and direction, especially when things get tough. It's not just about having a goal; it's about knowing the deeper meaning behind it. Why does it matter to you? Why should it matter to others? If your vision doesn't resonate personally, it'll lose its power, and you'll lose your motivation when obstacles arise.

Your vision doesn't have to be perfect from the start. When I began writing, I had only a general idea, but the details came as I moved forward. You need a guiding point to avoid chasing distractions that don't align with your purpose. Think of it like heading out on a road trip without knowing your destination—you'll just end up driving in circles, wasting time and energy.

> *Your vision gives you purpose and direction. What is your 'why'?*

A strong vision helps you filter out distractions and stay centered. Every time I got bogged down by self-doubt or perfectionism, I reminded myself why I was writing this book. It wasn't about me—it was about the people who needed to hear this message. That vision pulled me back to the keyboard every time I wanted to quit.

Your vision will evolve as you do, but its core purpose remains solid. It's your anchor when everything else is shifting. At the end of the day, your vision isn't just a goal—it's a statement of what you believe in and what you're working toward. It's what sets your story apart. So before you take any action, sit with your vision. Understand why it matters to you, and let that guide every decision from here on out.

Clara, a small business owner, had plenty of ideas but no clear vision. Once she clarified what mattered—providing eco-friendly products that made a real impact—her business took off. The clearer her vision became, the easier it was to make choices, as every decision was informed by her 'why'.

Step 2: Focused Action

Once I had a clear vision, it was time to stop thinking and start doing. But action without a strategy? That's just spinning your wheels. So, I focused on small, intentional steps every day instead of trying to tackle everything at once. Some days, it was about creating content and other days, it was refining and clarifying.

Strategy also requires flexibility. The writing didn't always flow smoothly, and I had to be okay with switching gears. When I hit a block, I'd switch to research or outlining instead. The key was to keep momentum, even when progress didn't look exactly how I had planned.

Focused action is knowing what needs your attention right now. For me, that meant starting with the chapters that felt clearest in my mind. Instead of keeping to a strict order, I followed where inspiration led, which helped me stay productive without feeling the enormity of the project.

Chapter 11: Craft the Story That Only You Can Tell

Maya, a marketing consultant I worked with, had a similar realization. She was juggling too many projects at once and feeling stuck. Once she narrowed her focus to the one with the biggest potential impact, everything shifted. By channeling her energy into what truly mattered, she not only moved her business forward but also found a rhythm that boosted her productivity across the board.

Strategic action is about showing up consistently and working on the things that matter most. It's not about rushing through tasks to check them off the list—it's about making deliberate progress, even if it's just one small step at a time.

Step 3: Sharpen Your Edge

As I moved deeper into writing, I realized that the person who started this project wasn't going to be the same person who finished it. Writing something meaningful requires more than just sitting down and typing—I had to upgrade my skills as I went, whether that meant improving my writing or learning how to better structure my ideas.

Growth forces you to confront your limits, but upgrading your skills allows you to push beyond them. There were moments when I struggled with words, but instead of staying stuck, I used those moments to improve. Seeking feedback, trying new approaches, and refining my communication were all chances to sharpen my edge.

Take Elon Musk as an example—he didn't start as an expert in every field that he's now involved in, but his dedication to learning allowed him to lead across industries like tech, energy, and space exploration. It's that mindset of continuous skill development that keeps you sharp.

Upgrading your skills is more than just acquiring new knowledge; it's about staying committed to improving and adapting. By the time I finished this book, I wasn't just a better writer—I was more effective and confident in my abilities. The willingness to continually sharpen your edge is what fuels long-term success, no matter the goal.

Step 4: Curate Your Space

When I started writing, I realized I needed an area that allowed me to focus and create, which meant a tidy space with limited distractions. That might look different for you, but your environment has to support your most productive self.

Your environment goes beyond the physical space; it's also about the people, conversations, and content you engage with. I knew constant distractions and negativity would block my creativity, so I carved out time, set boundaries, and built an environment that promoted mental clarity.

Knowing yourself helps you identify the ideal space, and sometimes, it's not the usual setup. I recorded content while pacing around my garage because movement helps my ideas flow. The same routine won't work for everyone, and that's okay—whether it's pacing or finding a quiet coffee shop, the key is creating an environment that keeps you grounded.

Chapter 11: Craft the Story That Only You Can Tell

Lisa, a graphic designer I worked with, struggled with the chaos in her home office. After rearranging her space, adding plants, and setting boundaries, her productivity soared. The clutter had been as much mental as physical, and once she cleared it, her creativity took off.

Take a look at the people around you. Are they pushing you to grow or pulling you into your comfort zone? While writing this book, I leaned into conversations with people who supported my vision and stepped away from those who drained my energy. Your relationships are part of your environment—if you're surrounded by people who don't support your dreams, it becomes much harder to move forward.

Optimizing your environment isn't just about clearing your desk or turning off your phone—it's about creating the conditions where you can thrive. Be intentional about the space you create—physically and mentally. When your environment supports your goals, everything flows more naturally, and progress feels less like a struggle.

Step 5: Master Your Mindset

The hardest part about this book was managing what was going on in my head. When I sat down to write, doubts and insecurities crept in. I didn't have the luxury of letting them take up permanent residence, so I did daily mental housekeeping. No matter how strong your goals or actions are, if you're not handling those internal battles, it's easy to get thrown off course.

Turn Your Story Into Business Gold

I'm the kind of person who jumps into the deep end when an opportunity presents itself. Of course, that kind of drive comes with its challenges—doubt and overwhelm can sneak in when things don't go as planned. That's when I rely on practices to keep my mind and emotions in check. Tapping into what shifts your energy or makes you smile is key to pulling yourself out of that emotional bog before it drags you down.

Susan, a small business owner I worked with, faced self-doubt when her sales slowed. Rather than letting that doubt take over, we focused her energy on product development—something that energized her. By shifting her attention to what sparked joy, she regained her momentum and moved forward with a renewed sense of purpose.

Managing your mind and emotions is what keeps you moving forward. It's the difference between giving up when things get tough and pushing through to the other side. Writing this book was a practice in trusting myself, staying connected to my vision, and believing I could figure it out along the way. Mastering your mindset is all about trusting that you can handle whatever comes next, no matter how unstable the ground feels.

Your mind is your most powerful tool, but it can also be your biggest obstacle. Mastering your mindset isn't about eliminating emotions—it's about learning to live with them while staying focused on the bigger picture.

These five steps? They aren't just something I coach—they're what I live by. Every client I work with, from entrepreneurs to executives, goes through these steps to

Chapter 11: Craft the Story That Only You Can Tell

own their story and create their version of success. Whether you're building a business, writing a book, or taking on something big, these steps will keep you grounded and moving forward.

Your Story is Your Strategy

By now, it should be clear—your story isn't just part of what you do; it's at the heart of everything. Whether you realize it or not, your story is the lens through which people see you, your business, and the value you bring. In a world where everyone's bombarded with messages, it's your story that cuts through the noise.

And here's the thing: your story isn't just a nice-to-have—it's your strategy. It's how people get to know you, understand what you stand for, and decide if they vibe with what you offer. Think of it as the language of your business.

When your audience hears your story, they should see themselves in it. It's not just about what you do; it's about addressing their challenges and aspirations—and showing them how your story provides the solution they need.

Effectively sharing your story is everything.

When you get clear on your story, it becomes the compass for everything you do in your business. Every opportunity, every decision—whether it's a marketing move, a new product, or a partnership—gets filtered through your story.

Does it align with who you are? Does it fit the narrative you're building?

That's the heart of storytelling as strategy—it's not about you; it's about your audience and how your story helps them live better, easier lives.

How to Create a Story That Resonates

At the heart of it, telling a story that hits home follows the same structure every time—whether you're crafting a pitch or writing a speech. It's all about having a clear framework and a goal. The difference? A pitch is short and sharp, while more time gives you space to dig deeper, pull on those emotional strings, and create connections. But the bones stay the same—you're still leading your audience through a journey, making sure they're with you every step of the way. At every point, ask yourself: "Why does my audience need to hear this?" That simple question will keep you on track.

- **Beginning:**

You need to grab attention from the first line. Even if your audience is committed (like a live crowd), you can't afford to let their minds wander. Start by painting a vivid picture of a struggle or problem. Layer in examples or smaller stories for context. Introduce yourself, the situation, and the challenge—this sets the foundation. From the start, you want them to feel seen and connected to your story, like it could be their own.

Chapter 11: Craft the Story That Only You Can Tell

- **Middle:**

This is where the magic happens. In a longer story, you get to dig into the obstacles, challenges, and those little "aha!" moments. You want your audience to be curious—how did you handle the roadblocks? What decisions shaped the journey? This is the heart of your story, where the stakes feel real and your growth starts to show. Keep them hooked by letting them into the process.

- **End:**

The conclusion isn't just about the win—it's about showing your transformation. It's not enough to say, "I succeeded." You want to show how you changed and evolved through the journey. What did you learn? How did the challenges shape you into the person or business you are today? This is where the audience can see the possibility of their own breakthrough.

- **Lesson:**

No great story is complete without a takeaway. This is where you reflect on what you learned and how those lessons can apply to your audience. In your story, the lesson is the moment of clarity—the point where everything clicks for both you and the people listening. You're drawing the thread from your personal experience to a universal truth, something that makes the story resonate on a deeper level.

- **Call to Action (CTA):**

Every story needs a next step. Without a CTA, your story feels unfinished. What do you want your audience to do next? What should they take away? Whether it's a literal action—like signing up for something—or an internal reflection, your CTA ties the whole story together and gives your audience direction. It's the bridge between your journey and their own.

This structure—beginning, middle, end, lesson, and CTA—gives your story a solid backbone, ensuring your audience stays with you every step of the way. While you can play around with how you tell it, sticking to this framework keeps your story clear, relatable, and impactful.

Learning from Great Storytellers

One of the best ways to sharpen your storytelling game is by watching the pros in action. You don't have to copy them, but you can study how they captivate an audience and incorporate their techniques into your own style. Whether it's a TED Talk, a book that really speaks to you, or even your favorite YouTube storyteller, pay attention to how they blend vulnerability, emotion, and purpose. Their delivery is just as important as the words they use.

Watch for how they use pauses, how their body language reinforces their message, and how their tone shifts to match the mood. These aren't tricks to replicate but tools to adapt to your own style. The goal is to find what works for you, so you can create that same level of connection with your audience.

Chapter 11: Craft the Story That Only You Can Tell

The beauty of storytelling is that it's not about perfection. It's about showing up, being present, and letting your voice carry the weight of your experience. You've got your own story to tell, and by learning from the best, you can refine how you share it—boldly, and with intention.

Conclusion: Stepping into Your Story

This is where it all comes together. After everything you've learned and the steps you've taken, there will be moments when you stand in front of your audience, your clients, or even just yourself, and think: *How do you like me now?* These are the moments where you prove—to yourself and everyone else—that you were capable all along.

Writing this book was one of those moments for me. I had doubts, just like you probably do, but I kept moving forward. And now, here I am, telling you that you can do the same. You can take your story, your struggles, and your growth, and turn them into something powerful—something that not only transforms your life but inspires others to do the same.

This journey isn't about proving others wrong; it's about proving yourself right. It's about standing firm in your story, believing in your voice, and never giving up on what you know to be true. Crafting your story isn't just about business—it's about showing up for yourself in the boldest, most unapologetic way possible.

When I set out to write this book in 45 days, I wasn't sure I could pull it off. But I knew one thing for sure: I wasn't alone. I was guided by the same principles I've shared with you throughout this journey—believing in your vision, taking strategic actions, continuously evolving, and managing the doubts and emotions that inevitably arise.

Your story is your strategy. It's your foundation, your guide, and your key to connection. But more than anything, it's your proof. Proof that you can overcome obstacles, push through doubt, and build something meaningful. Your story isn't just about what's happened to you—it's about what you do with it.

You have that same strength within you. You have everything you need to create your own *"how do you like me now"* moments—whether in business, life, or even a single, powerful conversation. Your story is a reflection of your resilience, your belief in yourself, and the unique message only you can bring into the world.

And when you reach that point—when you stand there with your story fully realized—you'll have your own *"how do you like me now"* moment. That's when you know you've taken control of your narrative. That's when you know you've written the story only you could tell.

Key Takeaways

1. **Own Your Story:** Your story isn't just part of your brand; it's the foundation. Use it strategically to connect with others and build something real.

2. **Stay Aligned:** A clear vision keeps you focused and grounded, helping you make decisions that move you forward. Stay aligned with your purpose.

3. **Take Focused Action:** Consistent, intentional steps—no matter how small—will move you closer to your goals. Progress is built through deliberate action.

4. **Sharpen Your Mindset:** Your mindset is your most powerful tool. Train it daily to overcome doubt and stay connected to your bigger picture.

Mindset Shifts:

1. **Embrace Growth:** You don't need all the answers upfront. Growth is a process—be willing to evolve as you move forward.

2. **Trust Your Process:** Obstacles are part of the journey. Trust that each challenge is an opportunity to refine your story and get closer to your goal.

3. **Keep Moving:** Progress isn't always linear. When doubts arise, focus on what you can control and keep taking steps toward your vision.

Action Steps for Crafting Your Unique Story:

1. **Reflect on your pivotal moments**: Take time to identify the key experiences in your life or business that have shaped who you are today. These moments will form the foundation of your story.

2. **Align your story with your vision**: Make sure your story reflects the bigger vision you're working

toward. It's not just about the past—it's about using your story to move you closer to your goals and showing others where you're headed.

3. **Take strategic action**: Don't let your story just sit there—use it to drive purposeful action. What steps are you taking to move toward your vision? Your story should fuel those actions and keep you on track toward your goals.

4. **Practice and share**: Share your story through different platforms—whether it's in conversations, on social media, or in speeches. Refine it as you go, but don't wait for it to be perfect before putting it out there.

If you haven't yet gotten your complimentary companion Workbook to go deeper and actually write our your thoughts, shifts, and steps, scan the code to get it now:

Additional Resources

Sometimes, it's great to have the information and start testing it out to see what develops.

Most of the time, it's even better to get personalized input and gain real-time insights from someone who *knows* and is walking the walk.

That's what you get when you connect with Leslie and become part of her world. Because she has a true passion to help you succeed!

Leslie offers a range of resources to help you grow at www.wildwomanmarketing.com/resources.

About the Author

Leslie Capps is an international best-selling author, speaker, and strategic consultant who's bringing storytelling to new heights—including a debut at the Oscars. Known for her talent in transforming untold stories into business gold, Leslie helps entrepreneurs rise from invisibility to build brands that resonate, connect, and thrive.

Her journey has been as adventurous as it is impactful. From running a multicultural center to leading sea kayak tours on the Yukon River in Alaska and, owning a ranch, Leslie's experiences add depth to her approach, infusing her work with grit, resilience, and a bold perspective on success. A lifelong outdoor enthusiast and fierce advocate for women, she's committed to the philosophy of *No Entrepreneur Left Behind*, guiding purpose-driven business owners who are ready to make a memorable impact.

Through her courses, speaking, and consulting, Leslie is redefining the business landscape, empowering others to stand out by owning the story only they can tell. For her, true success is rooted in authenticity, impact, and the connections that only a well-told story can create.

Thank You!

Thank you so much for reading *Turn Your Story Into Business Gold*. I can't wait to hear how it transforms your interactions and your business!

If you found this book valuable, would you kindly leave your honest review on the book page and share it with someone else who would benefit?

It would mean so much to me and help me reach even more readers.